ORCHIDS
for All

How to choose and care for your plants

ORCHIDS
for All

Jörn Pinske

Contents

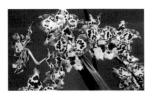

Introduction

Orchids – a very special family

▶ Advice on cultivation is often unclear. Are orchids really inedible? How much light do they require?

Orchids can now be bought almost anywhere, and are often found near the vegetables at the supermarket – ready-wrapped, tightly packed in a pot, easily damaged – yet these really are orchids. They are also available in florists, appealingly displayed in glass vases or designer containers, sometimes decorated with brightly coloured ribbons. And of course you can buy them in specialist orchid nurseries, usually as highly valued, sought after collectors' items.

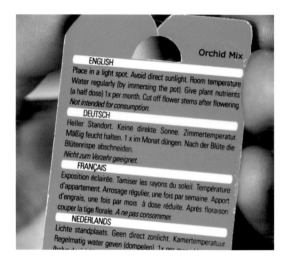

Nowadays, orchids are 'cheap', everyday purchases, but they are also valuable objects of beauty and elite plants for collectors. In any case, they remain something of a mystery. Are they actually parasites? Or even carnivorous plants? And are tropical orchids getting rarer? All these questions are answered here, and these answers explain how we can all grow and cherish orchids as something rather special, despite their wide availability.

History

Millions of plants have been brought to Europe since the Heidelberg professor Tabernaemontanus (Jacob Diether) described the first American orchid in his herbarium of 1588. The first introductions were exclusively from

▶ The variety of orchids available is impressive, but the quality is not always good. That can lead to problems even if you care for them properly.

the New World, with later finds from Asia and Africa. The motive was not always 'botanical' interest, but as often as not burning enthusiasm, even greed. Frederik Sander, originally from Bremen, provides a good example of such passion. After years travelling in Germany, Belgium and England, he established a nursery in St Albans in 1885, which soon became one of the world's major orchid importing businesses. Although he himself never left Europe, he sent plant collectors all over the world, and as many as 23 adventurers collected in the natural forests for Sander. However, 'collected' is a word that needs some expansion. The collectors frequently simply felled trees to reach the orchids growing high in the branches. Thousands of giant forest trees met this fate, and some Philippine islands were completely plundered as masses of orchids were removed. However, with the transport in those days, only a few reached Europe as viable plants, and almost all of these died soon afterwards in the (mainly English) greenhouses, because no one knew how to look after them.

The collectors too suffered privations. Many came to an early end in the tropics, or returned home ill. One of Sander's orchid hunters, Wilhelm Micholitz, wrote to his employer from the jungles of Vietnam: 'Here it is difficult to bring things down from the trees, as the trunks are alive with red beetles which deliver fierce bites.' He did, however, manage to put an unusual specimen of *Dendrobium phalaenopsis* var. *schroederiana* from New Guinea up for auction on 16 October 1891. He discovered it at a native burial ground, where one of the orchids was growing around a human skull, making the auction somewhat macabre. We still hear fascinating stories involving orchids. A newspaper story ran under the headline: 'No more orchids for Yang Bin'. Yang Bin came from a poor family in Nanjing, but in his youth he became the second richest person in China, with an estimated fortune of 900 million US dollars. In 1989 he invested 10,000 dollars in an apparently very lucrative textile company, and in 1994 he returned home with 20 million dollars, and rapidly increased the wealth of his firm, Euro-Asia-Group, by exporting orchids and cut flowers. But in order to make such a huge fortune he had to bribe some local politicians, and this eventually led to him being jailed for 18 years.

▲ This beautiful orchid illustration, originally hand-painted, is from an early book about orchid cultivation by F. W. Burbridge (1882). This is the impressive *Disa grandiflora* (syn. *D. uniflora*) from South Africa. Successful cultivation of this species is a real achievement.

Botany and cultivation

Most orchids come from the warmer regions of the world, but there are also some from temperate latitudes. These are the so-called terrestrial orchids; species whose top-growth dies back over the winter, just like other herbaceous perennials. Unbelievably, almost one in every ten flowering plants is an orchid – there are probably more than 30,000 species! Then there are the many hybrids, which include most of the orchids grown as houseplants, and these are often easier to grow than the original wild forms.

Epiphytic orchids

On 12 October 1492, Christopher Columbus reached the New World. He landed in the Bahamas, on an island known by its inhabitants as Guanahani, and which he named San Salvador. In his diary entry for 16 October he wrote: 'I noticed many trees, very unlike our own, amongst which were some with very different twigs growing from the same branch, giving an odd appearance…so that five or six completely different species grew side by side on one and the same tree.' Thus Columbus was the first European to describe epiphytes. The word epiphyte comes from the Greek *epi* = on and *phytos* = plant. Such plants are sometimes referred to as air plants. Epiphytes escape the intense competition of the forest floor, where faster-growing plants would overwhelm them, and this habit allows them access to the light they need to grow. They derive their nourishment mainly from rainfall and organic deposits. Estimates indicate that about 10 per cent of all land plants are epiphytes, and these include many ferns and bromeliads, as well as some 70 per cent of all orchids. Other orchids, such as slipper orchids and bee orchids, are terrestrial, that is they grow in the soil. Some grow on rocks (lithophytes), and some live on dead and decaying material (saprophytes). The latter cannot make their own food, as they have no green leaves. Instead they gain their nourishment from a relationship with fungi, as do many other orchids in the initial stages after germination.

► Many plants, notably orchids, ferns and bromeliads, grow epiphytically. However, they are not parasitic, but gain the advantage of increased light. This tree from a montane rainforest is festooned with epiphytes.

Special characteristics

The orchid family evolved some 120 million years ago, making it a relatively young plant family; it also exhibits variable forms. Orchids also display varied survival strategies, to the continued surprise of botanists. For example, an orchid has recently been discovered in Australia that gives off exactly the same scent (sexual pheromone) as female wasps in order to attract the males of the species. The male wasps follow the scent to the orchid flower, and then attempt to copulate with it, pollinating the plant in the process. This orchid is dependent upon a single wasp species for its survival. Many orchids imitate the shape and colour of a female insect, or produce chemicals attractive to more than one species of insect. In some cases the flower is almost invisible to the human eye, but lasts for weeks. Other orchids 'show off' through shape, size or colour. Almost all orchids are adapted to animal (mainly insect) pollination, and ants play a major role. Orchids announce their presence mainly through their flowers, using a huge range

◄ The pouch of a slipper orchid is actually the lip of the flower, and is a sophisticated trap. The escape route for insects leads them past the pollen and stigma, thus bringing about pollination.

of colour, shape and fragrance to attract pollinators. Clearly this can only work in the long term if the visitors find something worthwhile, in this case usually nectar – a tasty, nourishing sugar solution. This attractive offering is more than a free meal, and serves to achieve the transfer of pollen from one flower to another. Orchid pollen sticks to the visiting insect as a packet ready for despatch that can then be delivered direct to the stigma of the recipient. The so-called lip usually acts as a landing stage and signpost.

What the orchid has to offer depends on the pollinating insect. Thus perfumes attract bees by day, or at night moths, which are attracted to very sweet scents. Unpleasant (to us) scents attract flies. As for flower colour, bees like yellow or blue, but not red, while flies prefer dull brown or purple. Flowers pollinated by moths are often white, as colour is not important at night.

◄ The nectar guides are clearly visible on the lip of this *Cattleya*. They lead the insect direct to the nectar source, and are often yellow, or reflect UV-light, to which many insects are sensitive.

The shape of the flower is also an adaptation: it can be tubular, bowl-shaped or a beautiful slipper-like trap. The insect is attracted to what seems a safe landing site (the lip), but which is actually a slippery trap. The insect that falls into the pouch may have pollen on it already, and also receives pollen from the heart of the flower. The route back to freedom involves brushing past the stigma, thus pollinating the flower.

Flower structure

Despite wide diversity, the basic orchid flower consists of three petals and three sepals. These are always arranged so that a central line divides the flower into two mirror-image halves, meaning that the flower is bilaterally symmetrical, or zygomorphic. But this does not in itself allow a botanist to identify a flower as an orchid. The distinguishing feature is the column ('columna'), which projects upwards from the base of the petals at the centre of the flower and is formed from the stamens (often fused together) and stigma. The central petal is usually a different shape from the others. This is called the lip ('labellum'), which varies greatly in shape, colour and size between different orchid species. In the slipper orchids it has an inflated appearance, but in some it is small and inconspicuous, in many cases being fused with the column. The lip sometimes has fleshy raised areas differing in colour, often darker or paler, the so-called pollen- or nectar-guides.

Nectar ensures that the pollen is not all eaten but is transported, unnoticed, to exactly the right position and is transferred to the stigma of the next flower visited. The stigma has a particularly sticky surface to which the pollen attaches firmly.

It is important to know that orchid pollen is readily dispersed, after which the flower fades quickly. Therefore you needs to be careful not to lose the pollen, especially when moving *Oncidium* and the cambrias. The state of the flowers is not important in caring for orchids; the vital point is to encourage them to flower at all. In the wild, orchids flower to coincide with the activity of their pollinators, and this depends on season, temperature and rainfall.

► Every orchid flower is unique, but they all have the same fundamental structure, though they may vary widely in size and colour.

Sepal (dorsal sepal)

Column (columna)

Petals

Lip (labellum)

Pollinia

Sepals

The roots

Epiphytic orchids have aerial roots, of which there are a number of different sorts. Some roots extend into the open air, others grow into the growing medium, while others have a double function of support and nourishment. The actual root always has a spongy, whitish covering, the **velamen**. This consists of dead porous cells that suck up and store water like a sponge, thus enabling orchids to survive as epiphytes. In **terrestrial orchids** the velamen is replaced by hairs on the underground roots. The root tips are always smooth and usually fleshy. **Aerial roots**, which can be up to two thirds of the total bulk of the plant, are smooth and round at first with a yellow or green, sometimes reddish, tip, the green being chlorophyll. The green root tips grow towards the light, and require both light and air. Warmth around them encourages growth. Cold conditions, including damp cold caused by overwatering in a pot, inhibit their growth and may even kill them. When aerial roots meet a firm substrate they change and become **supporting roots**. These attach themselves so firmly that it is impossible to remove them undamaged. Some orchids also develop **nest roots**. These are upwardly growing lateral roots. The 'nests' or 'baskets' that result accumulate plant and animal remains, such as dead leaves, etc., which serve as a source of nutrients.

At the centre of the orchid root is the translocation system (vascular bundles), surrounded by a thin tissue (endodermis), covered by the outer tissue with its corky surface (exodermis), and the outermost velamen (epidermis). The porous cells of the outer layers carry water and any dissolved nutrients to the translocation system. This central

◄ Orchid roots bind tightly to the substrate, anchoring the plant through storms and rain.

translocation system is important not only for moving water and nutrients around the plant: its turgidity (even when inactive) gives the plant stability. Development of new roots signals the start of the orchid's growing phase, the shoots appearing later. Orchids live, at least some of the time, in symbiosis with a fungus, usually referred to as a **mycorrhiza**. One advantage of this relationship is that the very thin fungal threads can infiltrate the substrate more effectively than roots and can therefore gain better access to the meagre supply of nutrients. Orchid roots are very sensitive and react immediately to unsuitable conditions. At first they stop growing, and then, if the conditions do not improve, they die. The key to good orchid cultivation is a plant with plenty of roots.

◄ The green root tip shows that the aerial root is healthy. Behind the tip is the mainly grey 'velamen', which is an absorbent sheath.

Pseudobulbs and leaves

The leading shoot of an orchid, with its leaves, either grows continually upwards, or sends out side shoots each year at the start of the growing season. There are two basic types of orchid growth: *monopodial* (single shoot) and *sympodial* (many shoots). Monopodial orchids have an erect shoot and grow in one direction, with the lower parts sometimes dying later in the year. The leaves, usually in two rows, develop between the nodes, and the flowers appear later in the leaf axils. Sympodial orchids have a horizontal (creeping) shoot, from which side shoots grow vertically upwards. The familiar moth orchids (*Phalaenopsis*) are a good example of the monopodial habit, with no resting phase. Slipper orchids on the other hand show sympodial growth. Parts of the shoot may thicken as storage organs (known as pseudobulbs). A pseudobulb has one or two leaves and terminal (acranthous) or lateral (pleuranthous) flower buds. All orchids with pseudobulbs have a variable dormant period.

This dormant period is a response to the climatic conditions of the original habitat. In the case of hybrid orchids, of course, this rhythm is completely disrupted. However, it is always true that an orchid that is not growing is dormant, and failure to manage dormancy correctly is one of the commonest problems in growing orchids.

Orchid leaves are varied: some are soft, some almost succulent like those of cacti. But basically they serve the same functions as the leaves of other plants.

How orchids grow in the wild

Some orchids live in the tropical coastal regions of South America, Asia and Africa, notably in the basins of the Congo and Amazon. Here the climate is moist, warm and tropical, with daytime temperatures of around 35°C (95°F), and little cooling overnight. In the rainy season there are regular downpours in the afternoons, and the dry period is normally short. The orchids are therefore wet, even at night, and at other times get desiccated by the sun. Air currents prevent them going mouldy at night – and this needs to be imitated by the use of a ventilator when orchids are grown in a greenhouse or in a glass cabinet. **Tropical orchids** from these climates can be grown in heated greenhouses. Yet more than 60 per cent of all orchids are from **temperate regions**.

► The storage organs ('pseudobulbs') vary in shape, and are usually surrounded by bracts. From left: pseudobulbs of *Wilsonara*, *Coelogyne* and *Cattleya*.

Vertical climate zones sometimes result in different conditions within the same geographical range, such as in the Andes and Himalayas. Plant labels that only tell you the country of origin are therefore not very helpful as the climate is so dependent on the altitude.

Most of these grow in mountain ranges, such as the Himalayas, the Malayan peninsula, Indonesia, New Guinea or in the Andes of South America. Here moisture comes from the rains that result from moist air being forced upwards by the mountains, or direct from clouds and mists. Orchids are quite at home in such cloud forests and this is a paradise for all epiphytes, which are distributed in different climatic zones according to altitude. But there are also rainy and dry seasons here, and even in the dry seasons there is mist at night and dew in the morning. Day and night temperatures may differ by as much as 10°C (18°F) and these conditions should be imitated when growing such species. It is also important to provide sufficient fresh air. Lastly, some orchids come from savanna or steppe regions between 500 m and 1000 m (1500 ft and 3000 ft), in gently hilly, lightly wooded areas. These so-called **cold-growing orchids** grow mainly on rocks (lithophytes) or epiphytically on trees along watercourses. They have to withstand a long dry period and often shed their leaves at the end of the growing period. In the growing period the days are hot and dry, and the nights cool, with a range of up to 20°C (68°F). In winter the temperature may fall to freezing. Plants from this zone are not suitable as house-plants; they require a dormant period in a cold greenhouse, and correct watering.

The **terrestrial orchids** are found in temperate zones and in cold regions, whether in Siberia, Europe, China, Japan, in North America or in higher regions of the Andes or Patagonia. Some – including some fine cultivars – are suitable for growing outdoors (**garden orchids**).

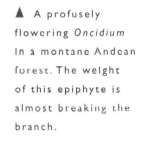

▲ A profusely flowering *Oncidium* in a montane Andean forest. The weight of this epiphyte is almost breaking the branch.

◄ A garden variety of slipper orchid, from the genus *Cypripedium*. Orchids such as this are often available from nurseries.

▲ Seed capsule of the orchid *Chysis laevis*, which has a many-flowered panicle. After pollination it takes several months to ripen.

Orchid reproduction

When an orchid flower has been pollinated it wilts relatively quickly, sometimes within hours. The ovary swells, the petals and sepals either drop off or shrivel, and the seed capsule develops. This may take several weeks, or even up to two years, after which the seeds are released. Moth orchids for example take 'only' nine months to ripen.

The embryo in the tiny seed has almost no food reserves and enters into a permanent or temporary symbiosis with root fungi (endotrophic mycorrhizae). Without the nutrients supplied by the fungus the seedling would not be able to grow further after germination. This fungus is hard to find, which may explain why orchids are quite rare, even in the tropics, despite the fact that one capsule may contain several million seeds! As the orchid grows it gradually loses the need for the fungus, although it sometimes persists and remains active in certain root cells. Plants cultivated at home, however, do not need this fungal symbiosis.

Records

The smallest orchid flower is about 2 mm ($\frac{2}{25}$ in) in diameter, while the largest measures almost 14 cm (5½ in) across. In height they range from a few millimetres, to rambling species several metres long (the famous aromatic vanilla, an orchid, holds this latter record). One species, with a shoot up to 5 m (15 ft) long, is probably the heaviest orchid. It is harder to judge the record for colours, but almost all colours are possible – white, red, blue, black or green, orchids cover the entire spectrum.

▶ A 5-cent coin looks gigantic next to the tiny flowers of this *Masdevallia* (above right). By contrast, the clambering vanilla orchid from Madagascar (right) grows to 15 metres (45 feet). The essential oils from the pods contain more than 35 fragrant components.

Modern propagation methods

Today the nutrients originally provided by the fungus can be given to the seeds in the laboratory (in a test-tube), and propagation is therefore possible without the fungus. Thus many plants can be grown from a single capsule. Plants propagated from one capsule are, however, not all alike, and this is true for all orchids, especially for intergeneric hybrids. Orchids with new colours, shapes and sizes can be selected from their progeny, and from these further new forms can be created. Attractive new varieties are given additional

cultivar names. Thus one form of moth orchid in the hybrid group Bright Peacock has the cultivar name 'Sweet Fragrance'. The correct designation for this plant is *Phalaenopsis* Bright Peacock 'Sweet Fragrance'.

To propagate such a particularly attractive plant it can be divided (in the case of sympodial orchids), or, in the case of a few (monopodials), by taking stem-tip cuttings. Another way is to use a very clever technique: **tissue culture**. This involves removing cells from a plant and stimulating these to divide. Further division is followed eventually by cell growth, and this gives rise to clonal progeny which are 100 per cent identical to the parent (meristem- or cell-cultured plants, sometimes called mericlones).

▲ Young plants of *Cattleya*, from about one year old (circular pot) to flowering size, five–seven years old. Orchids require a lot of patience in propagation and care.

Watering

Water quality

Water quality varies from place to place. For orchids the key factors are dissolved salts and acidity, including hardness, in other words the calcium and magnesium content. It is not simply enough to know whether the tap water is hard or soft: for orchid cultivation it is also important to know what makes the water hard, whether calcium or magnesium.

Fertilisers can be useful as these mostly contain no calcium, and, although magnesium is necessary, it can be harmful in large amounts. In general, soft water is better for orchids than hard, as one can then add the necessary calcium direct — about one teaspoon of calcium carbonate for a 10 cm (4 in) pot every six months, rather more for larger pots.

Water for orchids

Tap water should always be at room temperature and left to stand (chlorine takes at least 30 minutes to disperse). Hard water may be boiled and filtered or treated with a softening agent. Boiling removes so-called temporary hardness from the water, leaving calcium (lime) deposits, but for very hard water this is insufficient.

Using **rainwater** is another possibility, as long as this does not come off a dirty roof. Rainwater should be kept cool and dark, to limit

◄ The laboratory is increasingly where orchids originate, rather than in the tropics. This is where the seedlings or meristems spend their first months and grow protected in ideal conditions.

bacterial growth. With small orchid collections distilled (or desalinated) water can be bought and mixed with tap water, but orchids should never be watered with distilled water alone. In the case of very hard water, mix 1 part tap water to 2 parts distilled water, and for medium hard water use a ratio of 1:1. Water filters for making tea or coffee are also suitable for creating orchid water. These remove the damaging salts (mostly lime), and the filtered water can be used direct.

Correct watering

Success with orchids depends on correct watering. As epiphytes, they are not used to being over-watered, so it is no surprise that almost all losses are attributable to mistakes with watering, usually from too much water. Water leaches quickly through orchid compost, which is very free-draining compared with that used for other houseplants. Orchids need little water. Indeed as epiphytes they are adapted to such conditions and can also derive moisture from the air

▲ Moisture is best measured using a finger – if the growing medium feels cold (damp), do not water.

► Limp leaves and brown root tips are a sure sign of over-watering. It is commoner to water too much than too little.

NOTE Water requirement of orchids depends on:
- **Orchid species (origin – e.g. whether from steppe or rainforest)**
- **Epiphytic or terrestrial**
- **Size, succulent or soft leaves (transpiration surface)**
- **Size of pot (volume of growing medium compared with plant size)**
- **Whether restricted by container or not**
- **Type of container (clay pot or artificial, bark)**
- **Compost (with peat, bark, coir or expanded polystyrene)**
- **Position (ambient temperature, room, winter garden, greenhouse)**
- **Ventilation (open or closed)**
- **Season (growing or dormant period)**

through their aerial roots. Tropical rains are sudden, delivering relatively large amounts of water, and watering should imitate this regime. Although most water simply pours off, a healthy orchid plant is able to store some water in the velamen of its roots, from where it is slowly translocated to the rest of the plant. But this can only function if the roots are in a healthy condition.

Watering methods

We all possess a very simple instrument for testing – a **finger** – and this is where the gardener's legendary green fingers come into their own. Simply plunge your index finger into the compost, without looking. If it feels cool (damp cold), do not water. Also, if the pot feels light, then the substrate is dry and can be watered. If it is rather heavy it probably contains sufficient moisture. With practice, this becomes second nature, and you need never be misled by the top layer of compost. Even if this is quite dry, it can still be very damp deeper in the pot. Old composts retain water longer than fresh, loose compost. Within a week it generally dries out, and should then be watered, but if it remains moist longer, then water less often. In this context, transparent orchid pots are useful for observing the condition of the compost, and these are increasingly popular. For hydroculture, water level indicators can be helpful.

◄ Over-watering is also a danger with hydroculture. Water level indicators are often unreliable, and checking is essential.

Humidity

Air always contains water, and this is expressed as humidity. Air can only take up a certain amount of water, according to the temperature, and when this amount is reached we talk of saturated air, or air with 100 per cent relative humidity. Thus if the relative humidity stands at 50 per cent, the air can take up this same amount again.

Warmer air can hold more moisture than cooler air. In centrally heated houses the air is warmed quickly, especially in winter, but cannot take up water, as this is not usually available. Orchids can absorb water direct from the air via their aerial roots, but when the humidity is low, the leaves lose even more water to the air. The result is that orchids can become desiccated under such conditions if insufficient water has been taken up by the roots. Problems can also arise from high humidity, although this is seldom a problem in the home. In this case damaging fungi and bacteria can

grow quickly. Ideally, humidity levels should be in the range between 40 per cent and 80 per cent.

Misting

Humidity near plants can be measured with a hygrometer. If it is too high, it can be lowered by ventilation, but it is harder to raise humidity if it is too low. Rapid relief can be given by misting the plants, but they should never be left wet over night. It is best to use a fine mist spray, using soft rainwater at room temperature.

Another possibility is to place basins of water near to the plants. The surface area for evaporation can be increased by filling these with expanded clay pellets (e.g. LECA – lightweight expanded clay aggregate) or similar.

The basins should be cleaned regularly to discourage bacteria. Specialist orchid growers tend to use more complicated and expensive humidifiers.

▼ Misting devices use ultrasound to create tiny droplets of water which are carried in the air like real mist. The ultrasound is at a frequency that is harmless to people or animals.

Fertilising

Feeding orchids for growing and flowering

Orchids cannot survive simply on air and love alone. They require nutrients, like all living organisms, although epiphytic orchids are adapted to rather nutrient-poor conditions. They are able to profit from whatever is dissolved in the rainwater, including nutrients from atmospheric dust (which can be of Saharan origin, even in South America) and from the nitrogen in the air. However, atmospheric nitrogen is not generally available. Lightning strikes during storms oxidise nitrogen, which can then dissolve in the rainwater and benefit the plants.

Remains of rotten leaves, animal droppings and the like also accumulate in the substrate. But it is mainly from the rain that epiphytes gain a weak, yet constant supply of essential nourishment, and this needs to be taken into account when growing them. In short, orchids need nutrients like other plants, just rather less of them!

The right choice of fertiliser

Organic fertilisers such as bird droppings, bone or horn chips cannot be used by orchids until they have been decomposed by soil organisms, so in practice growers tend to use mainly inorganic fertilisers. Exceptions are liquid manures (plant or animal) and commercial liquid organic supplements.

Nutrients for orchids

Orchids need *nitrogen* (**N**) for growth of leaves and shoots. Insufficient nitrogen (rare) results in small, usually yellowish leaves; too much (much commoner) produces soft tissues and a dark green colour.

Potassium (**K**) promotes flowering, is good for the general metabolism of orchids and promotes powers of resistance. Insufficient potassium makes for soft tissues and arrested growth.

Phosphorus (**P**) promotes healthy root growth. Insufficient phosphorus causes a pink colour in the leaves, especially the undersides (although in *Phalaenopsis* this is normal).

Calcium (**Ca**) helps orchids take up other trace elements. It also promotes cell division and growth, especially of the roots.

Magnesium (**Mg**) helps with general metabolism and growth. Too little magnesium (rare) results in the leaves staying pale green.

Other trace elements important for healthy growth include *copper* (**Cu**), *iron* (**Fe**), *boron* (**B**), *zinc* (**Zn**), *molybdenum* (**Mb**) and *manganese* (**Mn**). These elements are effective even in tiny amounts. The precise role played by some of these remains unknown, but we do know that they are important.

Inorganic fertilisers (mineral or artificial) consist of salts of all the important elements required. These can be administered according to the individual needs of the orchid in question, or the season, by adjusting the dose.

Liquid orchid fertilisers are very easy to use and the instructions indicate the appropriate doses. **'Normal' liquid fertilisers**, used for most houseplants, should be diluted to at least half the recommended dose, or better not used at all. The so-called chelated fertilisers are a special case. These contain mineral salts associated with organic molecules. These fertilisers deliver the trace elements more effectively to the plant, and offer a particularly gentle and effective method of feeding orchids.

Fertilising individual plants

Whereas most plants start to grow in spring (when they need more feeding) and are then dormant in the winter (when they need less feeding), many orchids do not exhibit this rhythm. It is therefore important to adjust adding fertiliser to the growth cycle of the orchid to achieve optimal results. Orchids themselves indicate this: when a new shoot or leaf appears, this is the time to start feeding. You can either use a balanced fertiliser throughout the year, or use fertilisers with different nutrient compositions. Increase the amount slowly over a few weeks, and adjust the dose for each individual plant. A large, fast-growing plant will need more than a small, slow-growing plant. In the growing period a nitrogen-rich fertiliser should be used, which will stimulate vegetative growth, and this can be replaced by a potassium-rich feed, which helps

promote flowering. Dormant orchids should not be given fertilisers, while those with no dormant phase can be fed throughout the year, though it is still important to adjust the amount according to growth and flowering.

Feeding methods

The dose is indicated by the product. A good rule of thumb is to feed at every third watering, or at each watering but at less than half the

▲ A profusely flowering moth orchid needs plenty of feeding, but it is also possible to give it too much of a good thing.

recommended dose. To avoid salt accumulation the compost can be sluiced with pure water every three months (but not in the dormant phase). Orchids in baskets or mounted on bark should also only be given half the recommended concentration, as the lack of compost means that there is no buffer between the nutrients and the roots.

So-called foliar fertilisers should be sprayed on the undersides of the leaves, as there are more stomata there and uptake will be better.

Repotting and dividing

Orchids should only really be repotted for two reasons: either the container is too small, the plant having outgrown it, or the compost is exhausted. Unhealthy plants may also need repotting.

Propagation

Propagating orchids is a straightforward process. Sympodial plants can be divided, and monopodials propagated by taking cuttings or removing plantlets (keikis). If a plant has more than six pseudobulbs and two or more new shoots (growing in two directions), it can be divided. This not only produces an extra plant but also invigorates the orchid, and in some cases encourages flowering. Cut the

rhizome between the pseudobulbs with a sharp knife or secateurs. But take care to separate the plants very carefully, without tearing, by gently pulling them apart. Most sympodial orchids are easy to divide. Each plant should retain at least three active pseudobulbs, but if you need to maximise the progeny each pseudobulb can be used to create a new plant.

Propagation from backbulbs is another method. These can be removed when repotting and planted up separately. For most orchids a single pseudobulb is sufficient, although some require up to three. The compost should be sphagnum, peat or a mixture of polystyrene beads and wood shavings. Although not always successful, about 70 per cent of pseudobulbs develop fresh

► When dividing, as with this *Cattleya*, care should be taken – do not rip or break the plant, but instead make a smooth cut or gently pull apart, leaving at least three pseudobulbs on the new plant. Small sections and backbulbs can be retained for further treatment. Cut surfaces or open wounds should be treated with fungicidal powder to prevent infection.

Plantlets (keikis)

These sometimes develop instead of flowers on a pseudobulb or, in the case of *Phalaenopsis*, on the flower stalk, and they provide another method of vegetative propagation. Sometimes they develop as a response to poor cultivation. To survive, keikis need at least two leaves, and to have developed roots of sufficient length, a process that can take as long as a year and a half. The larger the plantlet, the better its chances of survival. Until then the plantlet can be sprayed with fertiliser to strengthen it. When large enough, or if the supporting stem dries out, it should be removed. For more information, see under the individual plant entries.

◄ Backbulbs can be used for propagation, as here with *Cattleya*. Simply place in sphagnum moss in a plastic bag, and keep light and warm (18–25°C/64–77°F), watch out for rot, and wait for new growth.

growth and can be potted up after developing roots.

Propagation from internodal cuttings is a neat method of reproducing orchids with elongated pseudobulbs, mainly *Dendrobium*. Green, leafless canes with at least three nodes are placed flat in a tray filled with a peat- or sphagnum-polystyrene mixture and kept at an even warm temperature. Longer canes can be cut into sections and the cut surfaces treated with fungicidal powder. Cover the dish with a cloth or plastic to raise the humidity, but ventilate regularly. After a few weeks the cuttings will develop new growth, and can be potted up after root development.

Monopodial orchids such as *Vanda* can be propagated using **stem cuttings**. This is helped by the production of roots on the upper third of the plant. Further tips can be found in the relevant plant descriptions.

◄ A keiki is clearly visible on this *Phalaenopsis* – note the new roots. This is now large enough to be grown as a separate plant. It may be simply removed and potted up.

Hints on repotting

When to repot: Generally, plants should be repotted when in full growth, when fresh shoots and root development are apparent. It is the plant itself, rather than the time of year, that determines the right time.

Before: Prepare the planting material and container and lay out drainage and binding material and a sharp pair of scissors. Water the orchids a day before repotting, and fertilise healthy plants. Dampen the new planting medium – it may help to spray the compost with a fine mist.

Afterwards: After an initial good soaking, the orchid should be sprayed after about 14 days. Plants with poor roots, or no roots at all, can be covered with transparent plastic film for eight weeks to reduce transpiration.

Composts

Orchids grow best when special composts are used, rather than normal pot plant composts. Epiphytes prefer an extremely free-draining material, one that allows plenty of air to reach the roots (aerial roots). The ingredients commonly used are

► Good orchid compost should contain components such as bark, peat and coco-chips or coir fibre.

Recipes for orchid compost

Type A (epiphyte mixture)
3 parts peat
2 parts bark
2 parts polystyrene beads/rockwool
1 part coir fibre

Fertiliser per 1 litre/1 pint:
4 g/$\frac{1}{16}$ oz calcium carbonate
2 g/$\frac{1}{32}$ oz horn chippings
0.5 g/$\frac{1}{128}$ oz complete fertiliser
0.5 g/$\frac{1}{128}$ oz trace nutrient fertiliser

<u>Note</u>: Universal, stable for 2 years.

Type B (terrestrial orchid mixture 1)
1 part peat (coarse)
1 part peat (fine)
1 part expanded clay, LECA, or loam
1 part bark
1 part polystyrene chips

Fertiliser per 1 litre/1 pint:
3 g/$\frac{1}{10}$ oz calcium carbonate
0.5 g/$\frac{1}{128}$ oz complete fertiliser
0.5 g/$\frac{1}{128}$ oz trace nutrient fertiliser

Type C (terrestrial orchid mixture 2)
3 parts peat
2 parts polystyrene beads
2 parts expanded clay, LECA, or loam

Fertiliser per 1 litre/1 pint: as for mixture 1

<u>Note</u>: Suitable for *Cymbidium*, *Zygopetalum*.

coarse peat, bark, coir, coconut chippings, polystyrene beads or rockwool, and sometimes perlite or expanded clay. All retain and store water and air. Bark is particularly nutrient-rich and contains more minerals than coconut or peat. Bark and peat also work well as buffers against the damaging effects of salts.

◄ ◄ Transparent pots make it easier to monitor growth and also promote root activity.

◄ Wooden baskets such as this are available, or can easily be made at home.

Containers for orchids

Artificial or clay pots? Most pots nowadays are made of plastic or other artificial materials. Clay pots are rarer, though they can yield better results due to their porosity. The advantages of plastic pots are that they are lighter, and retain neither water (damp cold) nor nutrients (salts can cause damage in dry conditions). They are also easier to keep clean. On the other hand, the heavier clay pots are more stable (especially useful for *Dendrobium*). But they also attract algae and retain bits of compost. Orchid growers are increasingly using transparent pots, which allow light to reach the roots, and also allow you to see how damp the compost is. Thus the roots can take part in assessment, especially in the case of *Phalaenopsis*. Many orchid enthusiasts make their own baskets, from wood or plastic.

Lastly, **epiphytes can be grown on bark**. Oak, beech, conifers with firm bark, cork oak or vine is suitable, and the orchids are tied to it, together with moss or coir fibre, rather than peat fibres (which are too acid). However, this method requires relatively high humidity. Strips of nylon stockings are suitable for binding, as this is elastic and does not damage the plant or its roots. In general, orchids do better as houseplants in pots rather than on bark. Those best suited to tying to bark are those that do not thrive in pots, such as those with many aerial roots (some monopodial species), or miniature orchids with very thin roots. This method of display is very labour-intensive, as they need frequent spraying. Good candidates are succulent orchids such as *Brassavola*, some *Oncidium* species and succulent dendrobiums that are adapted to light, dry conditions with a long dry phase.

▼ Orchids should not be tied too tightly (nylon stockings are useful for this), and their own roots will eventually lock them in place. Moss or coconut fibre can be used.

NOTE **Always make sure that water uptake** is optimal, whether the container is artificial, clay or ceramic. Plastic pots may be drilled at the base or lower third (holes not less than 8 mm/ ⅓ in diameter).

▲ Special pots are now available which deliver water in a more controlled way, thus benefiting the orchids, and this may be combined with the use of expanded clay pellets.

► Trays with a grille are very useful for orchid growing.

Position

Orchids need fresh air, but draughts can be dangerous, as for all houseplants, and should be avoided at all costs. Sudden cold or frost from outside must also be avoided. The following can also cause problems: old ripe fruit (which gives off ethylene), glue, paint, and smoke from cigars, cigarettes or from an open fire. As with all flowering plants, exposure to these can lead to bud drop or wilting. Orchids adapt to their site and should therefore be replaced in their original positions after cleaning windows or repotting. It is generally best to avoid moving them around too much.
Never spray orchids in full sunlight; they dislike the resulting rapid cooling from evaporation. They can however adapt to bright situations as long as they have enough time to acclimatise. All house orchids require relatively high humidity, and this can be a problem in centrally heated homes. But the humidity does not need to be increased throughout the

house, just in the immediate vicinity of the plants. This is where dishes of water can help, as discussed earlier. These can be purchased from orchid specialist outlets, or you can use window box trays. They should be filled with expanded clay pellets or LECA and then topped up with water. The orchids are then placed on top, but should not be allowed direct contact with the water. This can raise the humidity around the plants by some 30 per cent. A radiator beneath the shelf can help raise the humidity further.

Buying orchids

Hints as to what to watch for when buying orchids are given under the individual plant entries. Transport is also important. In spring, autumn and winter, orchids should be well packed for transport, and in summer they need to be shielded from direct sun. Never leave them for long periods of cold or heat inside a vehicle. They should also be moved with care as the leaves, roots or flowers are easily damaged. Every move means stress for the orchid. It is better to keep them too dry rather than too wet. Never over-water them.

How orchids are named

Identification should be easy, and one should always try and establish an orchid's identity. However, labels attached to orchids are very often misleading. These often simply say something like cambria orchid, or slipper orchid, or *Phalaenopsis*. There will usually also be notes on cultivation, often in more than one language, but nearly always vague: 'not too much light, but also not too little; not too much water, but also not too little…'

Each plant has a scientific name, and also often a common name as well. Thus botanists use the name *Paphiopedilum* rather than 'slipper orchid', often shortening this to 'Paph'. There may also be more than one common name, which can add to the confusion, and hints on cultivation may be associated with the wrong plant. Therefore always try and refer to the Latin name – genus and species.

For example: the slipper orchid *Paphiopedilum callosum* was imported in millions from Thailand and Vietnam. The first part of the Latin binomial is the genus, the latter indicating the species within that genus. There are also many naturally occurring forms of this species (in a range of colours), and these receive an extra name as varietas (var.). Thus *Paphiopedilum callosum* var. *sanderae* is a green-and-white form of the species. There are also hybrid groups, known as grexes, for example from a cross (indicated by ×) between *Paphiopedilum callosum* × *Paphiopedilum delenatii*. Hybrid groups are given a name, such as *Paphiopedilum* Madame Martinet. Particular selections within a hybrid group are normally designated by a further name in single inverted commas, such as *Paphiopedilum* Black Cherry 'Pink Crest'. Some names (e.g. Cambria) are applied to a whole range of hybrids, while some intergeneric hybrids are collectively gathered within *Odontoglossum*, for instance (see page 56). If you know the name of an orchid and wish to discover more about it, it is best to ask in a specialist outlet, or orchid society. The Internet is also very useful.

In addition to the many wild orchid species, there are now huge numbers of hybrids. Therefore we can only give a few examples here as a mere introduction to this wealth.

◀ *Paphiopedilum callosum* from Thailand has not only an interesting flower, but also decorative marbled leaves.

Phalaenopsis

Phalaenopsis – the moth orchids

Everyone knows the name *Phalaenopsis*. It is an orchid that copes extremely well with the conditions in most living rooms, and is also a parent species of many of the most important hybrids. There are about 70 species of *Phalaenopsis*, found growing wild from India to the Philippines and Australia. They are all epiphytes, with numerous aerial roots, stems up to about 30 cm (12 in) long, and large, broad, usually leathery leaves. The flowering stems arise from the axils of the lower leaves and can reach a length of up to 100 cm (39 in). They are often branched and bear a number of flower buds, mostly arranged in pairs, which open from the bottom upwards. For decades the most important species in cultivation has been *P. amabilis*, a white-flowered plant with relatively large flowers. The first time it was used for hybridisation was in England in 1866.

◄ *Phalaenopsis* **Hilo Lip** (= *P*. Hilo Beauty × *P*. Elaine Mishima). A notable feature of this famous orchid is the white lip. It can be obtained as a meristem.

▲ Most white varieties of *Phalaenopsis* can be traced back to *P. amabilis*. The flowers are long-lasting, and the lip may be yellow, white or red, depending on the variety.

◄ *Phalaenopsis* **Brother John** (*P*. Brother Delight × *P*. Brother Brungor). This produces a huge flower, up to 9 cm (3½ in) across, with an attractive red lip.

▼ *Phalaenopsis* **Golden Peoker
'Brother',** a hybrid from Taiwan. The
flowers look artificial and are very long-
lasting, but there are usually no more than
six to eight flowers in an inflorescence.

▲ Orchids in decorative displays with moss
or lichen are sometimes tricky to water
correctly. Use the finger test.

◄ Most colours
are available among
the many varieties
of *Phalaenopsis*.
Sometimes you
need a bit of
patience, or search
on the Internet.

The Variety of Phalaenopsis

◄ Varieties of *Phalaenopsis* differ not only in colour, but also in shape and size, texture, and durability. Such factors come from their forebears, which include some 70 species. Illustrated here: **Phalaenopsis Jewelers Art**.

► Most yellow *Phalaenopsis* last well. **Phalaenopsis Golden Leopard** (= *Phalaenopsis* Amboin × *Phalaenopsis philippinense*).

► **Phalaenopsis Salu Peoker** × **Golden Peoker** has very durable, waxy, rather stiff flowers. Care is as for all other *Phalaenopsis*. Large plants produce several flower stems.

34

◄ *Phalaenopsis* **Carmela's Pixie** has many, somewhat smaller flowers on a branching flower stem. The flowers are something of a 'novelty' and are reminiscent of the species *Phalaenopsis equestris*.

▲ This *Phalaenopsis* **Golden Circle** has the drooping inflorescence typical of the epiphytic habit that is common to all *Phalaenopsis*.

◄ Planters containing two or three different varieties of *Phalaenopsis* are quite popular. Although they may look attractive, they are tricky to grow, as the requirements of each may differ.

35

Cultivation

Temperature

The best temperature for *Phalaenopsis*
is between 18 and 25°C (64 and 77°F). By day,
with artificial heating, the temperature should
not fall below 20°C (68°F), while in summer,
with the warmth of the sun, moth orchids can
of course tolerate higher temperatures. The
night temperature, especially in winter, may
occasionally be allowed to drop to 16°C
(61°F), but never lower than this. At low
temperatures, it can happen that flowering

stems exude a sweet, sticky substance. In order
to stimulate flowers, a difference of about 5°C
(9°F) between the day and night temperatures
is necessary. The already long flowering season
can however be extended further by keeping
the plants fairly cool as soon as the first
flowers have opened, but the temperature
should not be allowed to sink below 18°C
(64°F). The principal flowering time is spring,
though *Doritis* species flower in summer. This
genus is often crossed with *Phalaenopsis* to
form hybrids. Because of the large number of
hybrids produced, varieties are now available
that can flower at almost any time of year.

Light

Moth orchids require a situation in partial
shade and without direct sunlight; west and
east-facing windows are especially suitable.
Next to a south-facing window, some
additional shading is necessary from March to
September. A directly north-facing situation is
mostly too dark. In order to test light levels,
an African violet should be placed there as a
trial plant. If this thrives in the situation and
comes into flower, then the light will also be
sufficient for *Phalaenopsis*. (An African violet
can, however, react to too much light. In this
case its sensitive leaves turn a reddish colour,
and the *Phalaenopsis* must be shaded
immediately.)

Humidity

Like all tropical orchids, moth orchids need
high humidity as far as possible. Therefore, it is
not sufficient just to water the pot. In order to
increase the humidity of the air round the
plants, it is best to stand them on shallow

▼ Not all examples
of *Phalaenopsis*
display such a
harmonious
relationship of
flower size and
stem length as
this. This is easier
to achieve in
mature plants.

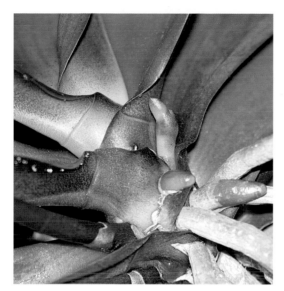

risen. Cold water on the leaves can even lead to buds dropping off. Before watering, either test the compost with the finger in the way described on page 18, or develop a definite rhythm in watering according to your experience and the surroundings. As each location is different there can be no single rule, either for the frequency of watering or the amount of water given. Generally you can say that if a *Phalaenopsis* is watered it should

◄ Growth buds are not always easy to identify, as initially they look rather like the root tips.

◄ To the left a normal, healthy leaf: firm in texture, and shiny. Next to it, to the right is one that is dull and crumpled. This is usually caused by too much water.

be done thoroughly. It does not matter if it is watered from above or if it is immersed in water, but any excess water should always be allowed to drain away.

The next watering should only take place when the compost below the surface has

trays, such as those available commercially for placing under window-boxes or pot-plants on balconies. The tray should be filled with expanded clay pellets or gravel. This enlarges the surface area and consequently the amount of evaporation. However, the pots themselves should not be allowed to come into direct contact with the water. For individual plants, larger pots can be used, and the *Phalaenopsis* stood inside on a layer of expanded clay pellets. In specialist shops, water vaporisers or indoor fountains are available which are equally suitable for improving the humidity of the air. Like all orchids, moth orchids do not grow in isolation in the wild but form plant communities. This should also apply when they are grown indoors. Plants with large, soft leaves, from which there is considerable transpiration, make particularly good companions – such as bromeliads, whose leaves form a funnel that fills with water.

Watering

Phalaenopsis, unlike many orchids, must never be allowed to dry out completely, nor can they tolerate an excess of water. Since at night the leaves should never be damp, they are best watered in the morning. In general, you should delay watering until the room temperature has

◄ Always follow the instructions when feeding, and always use less rather than more. Never feed unhealthy plants.

▲ **Repotting.** Slide the plant carefully from the pot. Remove compost. Cut away any rotten roots. Insert the plant into the new pot, which should not be too big. Add loose material for drainage, followed by the compost. Push the compost around the roots, but not too firmly, and finally, water.

► The appearance of a new central leaf on a *Phalaenopsis* indicates the start of the growing period. Time to repot.

become dry. As a rule this takes seven to ten days. In order to raise the humidity of the air, moth orchids should be misted (several times on warm sunny days, but then only with a small amount of water). For this purpose use a very fine spray and water at room temperature. Water should never be allowed to reach the new, inner leaves, particularly in the evening, since there is a danger of rotting.

Ventilation

Moth orchids need abundant fresh air to prevent insect pests, bacteria and moulds from becoming established and multiplying. The presence of soft, watery bacterial rot is often the result of inadequate ventilation. Of course, cold air must never blow directly on to the plants, since this leads to bud drop. This entails more than simply protecting the plants from frost, for even a drop in temperature of 10°C (18°F) can cause loss of buds and damage to leaves. Even draughts are harmful, especially when the current of air is colder than 14°C (57°F).

Feeding

The use of fertilisers should not be neglected, particularly in the case of hybrids. A standard orchid fertiliser should be applied, at every third watering.

Repotting and Compost

When the compost has been exhausted – easily recognisable by a slimy, mossy, or compacted surface – or the moth orchid simply has no room in the pot to expand, it is time to repot. Of course, you must always wait until a new inner leaf becomes visible.

Like all orchids, *Phalaenopsis* requires a special potting compost, and ordinary potting compost is not appropriate. For repotting, ready-mixed orchid compost can be used, so long as it is of good quality. Flat bags, which also feel soft, probably contain only a mixture of peat and fine bark, and this is really not a suitable compost for *Phalaenopsis*. But this can easily be improved or you can make a passable compost yourself (Compost Type A if you are mixing it yourself, see page 24). In addition to pieces of bark and charcoal, it is particularly advisable to add expanded polystyrene beads, so that the compost will retain water. Coconut fibre and chippings are also very suitable. When planting, choose coconut chippings or bark for the topmost layer to improve the look of the plant.

Phalaenopsis thrives very well in shallow containers. For healthy plants, the new pot should be not more than three sizes up from the old one.

Before repotting, cut back all damaged and rotten roots and, in the case of unhealthy,

weak plants, all the flowering stems as well. The base of the stem, if dry and devoid of roots, can also be cut away. Any new flowering stems and flowers are also best removed, since the plant will not have enough strength for their development.

First of all fill one-third of the pot with drainage material (polystyrene is suitable here too – simply break up clean packing material). Then place the plant in the centre and fill the pot with compost up to the lowest pair of leaves. After repotting, cover with plastic film or a transparent bag to retain any moisture lost by evaporation. For further hints, see page 22.

▶ A plastic bag supported by sticks acts as a mini-greenhouse for the first few weeks after repotting.

Expert Tips

1 **Buying**

Look at the general condition of the plant and its roots. It is better not to buy plants that are loose in their pots and only attached by the flowering stem, as well as those whose leaves are limp. The same may be said about plants bearing buds, i.e. no flowering stem should be carrying only a single bud. The best time to buy flowering plants is when a third of the stem is already in flower. In this state the orchid is most tolerant of being moved, avoiding the loss of buds, and will give the longest possible flowering time. Do not transport *Phalaenopsis* in a cold or a hot car, and never buy plants from places that are cold because of the air conditioning.

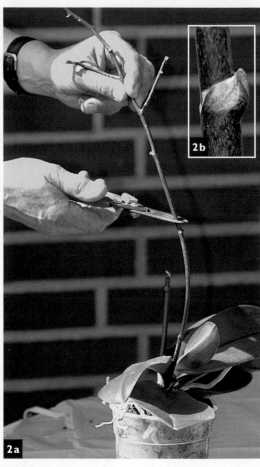

2 **Maintaining flowering**

Before the inflorescence begins to fade at the tip, certain *Phalaenopsis* have the ability to develop another flower from the so-called terminal bud. This does not look particularly attractive and it is better to encourage the plant to build a completely new flowering stem. Do not cut back the stem completely but cut it about 1 cm (½ in) above the second or third node (see inset **2b** on **2a**). Ensure that the stem is not crushed but make a clean cut. With luck a new and complete flowering

2c

than normal – though this should still be free-draining.

4 Can *Phalaenopsis* be kept with other houseplants?
Certainly, foliage plants can be used to provide shade and to keep the air humid.

5 Is it possible to put *Phalaenopsis* outside in summer?
This is not recommended, as the night temperature even in summer is frequently too low, so do not do this even for the week or two that you are away on holiday.

6 What to watch out for in the greenhouse
Cultivation under glass is really no different, though the amount of light and the humidity of the air are usually better. If there is an overhead watering system, it is better when repotting to place the *Phalaenopsis* at a slight angle so that excess water can run away easily. Staging benches are a highy effective method of display. If the greenhouse is not ventilated, a ventilator will be required to keep the air fresh. This will prevent mould and insect attacks. Gas heating systems with an open flame are not suitable for *Phalaenopsis*.

stem will develop from one of the nodes **2c** . The entire process will take about 90 days, so be patient!

3 Keikis
Plantlets, particularly in the case of small-flowered varieties, can sometimes develop on the flowering stem (usually without the plant coming into flower). They can also appear as a response to overwatering or too high a temperature. These are small offshoots, also known as keikis. This means no flowers are produced, but instead you get one or sometimes even several new plants. But you will need considerable patience for at least two leaves and several roots (about 5 cm/2 in long) are necessary for the plantlet to survive. And that can take a year or more! The larger the plantlet, the greater its chances of survival.
When an individual plantlet has appeared and/or the stalk on which it hangs is dry, cut the stalk above and below the plantlet (do not pull it off or cut it from the stalk). Put the plantlet with the remainder of the stalk into orchid compost. Use a small pot and a finer grade compost

3

► Plastic clips are useful for securing stems.

7 Staking

It may be necessary to support the flowering stem so that it does not snap under its own weight, particularly in the case of the large-flowered varieties. Use either natural or artificial bast or soft covered wire and stakes or split bamboo of adequate length. Stake with care, as it is the flowering stem's natural habit to hang down, and it will also look more impressive in this position. But if you want to prevent this, the stem must be fixed in two places. Never tie the stem too tightly, and always ensure there is a gap between the stem and the support to which it is attached.

8 Growing epiphytically

Where there is sufficient humidity in the air this is an effective method of display. In addition to the special clay tubes that are suitable for all epiphytes, moth orchids may be attached to cork, bark or pieces of tree fern. It is important to do this at the right time, when the plant is in active growth. Bast, cut-up nylon stockings or artificial strips are recommended as soft binding material. As a base, sphagnum moss, coconut fibre and fibrous peat (or a mixture of these) can be used. If the plant works free it should be re-attached. The roots or even the plants themselves must not be cut, nor should they be allowed to hang loosely down. Plants grown in this way need to be sprayed more frequently and supplied with low-salt nutrients.

7

9 If the plants are otherwise healthy, the temperature should be lowered to about 16°C (29°F) for three to four weeks. As the temperature drops, the plants will need less light and water. Flowering normally begins about three to four months after this treatment.

10 Bud drop

At low temperatures, lack of light (in winter or due to a sudden change in the weather), draughts, stress in transport or from ethylene (from smoke, fruits or exhaust fumes) can cause buds to drop off, and this often happens when the bud is about the size of a pea. The cause is frequently uncertain, and even owners of greenhouses (and professional gardeners!) are not immune from this. There is really no reason to panic. Just cut back the flowering stem to the third or fourth node and wait for the new inflorescence to develop (avoiding of course the possible causes of the problem).

11 Pests and diseases*

The main danger, apart from avoidable errors in cultivation, comes mainly from scale insects and mealybugs ㉘, ㉙ (see photo on right), various kinds of mite ㉝, ㉞ and also, more rarely, thrips ㉜. If moth orchids develop small brown patches which quickly get bigger and become transparent and moist, you should cut away the leaves at this point and reduce the humidity of the air and the frequency of watering. Plants that are rotten in the centre

10

◄ Effects of virus on a *Phalaenopsis* flower.

cannot usually be saved (see picture on page 136). Damage to roots and leaves can be treated with activated carbon (obtainable from a chemist), which makes it more difficult for germs to penetrate the plant ⑥–⑧. Fungus gnats are increasingly common 5. Make sure that air can penetrate the compost ①–③. Harmful problems include viruses ㊱ (see photo above), and more rarely snails ㉚. In addition, unfortunately, you will fairly often have to dispose of pea-sized buds ㉔.

Transporting plants wrapped in film may sometimes result in an attack of *botrytis* ㉕, but the damage may only be visible when you arrive home. Wilting of *Phalaenopsis* may be due to the following causes: too much water, too little water, too high a temperature, compacted compost, too much fertiliser, pest attack, too low a temperature, or too great a difference between day and night temperatures. From time to time, tools (secateurs, knives) for working on the plants should be sterilised (in a naked flame or in the oven at 240°C/460°F.) so that diseases are not passed on from one plant to another.

12 Hydroculture

Phalaenopsis are suitable for cultivation by this method since they are kept simultaneously warm and damp. But always wait for the new leaves to form in the centre of the plant before moving them. Never let the water rise beyond the maximum level, and always use liquid rather than slow-release fertilisers.

◄ Scale insects on a flower. These are more commonly found on the leaves.

*The numbers refer to the Appendix, page 135ff.

Miltonia

Miltonia –
the pansy orchids

▼ **Miltonia**
(*Miltoniopsis*)
Lycaena
'Stamperland'
was bred in England
in 1925.

These distinctive orchids (sometimes known as pansy orchids) all belong to the genus *Miltonia*, which nowadays includes a small group of six species formerly separated from the rest and called *Miltoniopsis*. The first hybrid, made in 1899, involved plants belonging to this group. In 2003 *Miltonia* cultivation occupied fifth place among all the orchids offered for sale, 1.2 million plants coming from the Netherlands alone. It is easy to distinguish a *Miltonia* from a *Miltoniopsis* – a *Miltonia* pseudobulb has two leaves, a *Miltoniopsis* pseudobulb has one. Hence, cultivated plants called *Miltonia* will usually have two-leaved pseudobulbs. All the species originate in tropical America, and the three that are the ancestors of most of the modern hybrids come from Colombia, Ecuador and Panama. There they live in hot, damp lowland (*Miltoniopsis roezlii*), in relatively cool, damp, cloudy forest (*Miltoniopsis vexillaria*), or in continuously damp tropical forest (*Miltoniopsis phalaenopsis*). The word that connects all these is 'damp', and dampness, in the form of rain, mist or dew, is present throughout the whole year. Other genera such as *Brassia*, with about 20 species native to tropical America, or *Oncidium* are now more frequently crossed with *Miltonia* and offered for sale as *Miltassia* or *Miltonidium*. Cultivation of these is closer to that needed for the intergeneric hybrids (see under that heading).

▶ **Miltonia Celle**,
is the most
successful German
hybrid of recent
years. From Celle
it has spread
worldwide.

46

◄ *Miltonia* **Alger 'York'** is a hybrid which demonstrates the common name 'pansy orchid'.

▼ *Miltassia* **Cairns 'New River'** is the result of a cross with *Brassia*. It has large, beautifully coloured and patterned flowers, reminiscent of coral fish of the Barrier Reef.

▲ *Miltonia* **Honolulu 'Warnes Best'** is a hybrid reminiscent of *Miltonia spectabilis* (var. *moreliana*). Very robust, and a good beginner's plant.

◄ *Brassia* **'Rex'**. These orchids mimic spiders to fool spider-hunting wasps. The flowers last six weeks or more.

47

Cultivation

Temperature, light and humidity

Temperatures over 30°C (86°F) are not suitable for these plants. In summer especially they should be kept fairly cool, which can be difficult to achieve. 14–16°C (57–61°F) would be ideal. Of course in winter the temperature can be 18–25°C (64–77°F) and they can then be grown alongside *Phalaenopsis*.

Even in summer they do not like too much light. In fact *Miltonia* requires even less light than the moth orchids. In summer it is possible to stand the plants outdoors in a shady place in the garden. A slightly reddish appearance to the leaves shows that the amount of light is sufficient, while red or pale yellow leaves indicate that the situation is too bright. If the intensity of light is too great, the sepals and petals will bend backwards. It is also preferable to keep miltonias in a somewhat shadier place after the buds have formed.

The humidity of the air should always be kept as high as possible. Without trays under the pots the plants will quickly dry out. When the air is low in humidity, use a fine spray on the plants several times a day, but let them dry off in between each spray.

Watering

Miltonias are not easy plants to water correctly and mistakes in their cultivation are only rarely tolerated. The compost must never be allowed to dry out, on the other hand an excess of water will inevitably lead to the onset of rot. So it is absolutely essential to ensure that there is good drainage. In summer, plenty of water will be required, but in winter, watering should be done more cautiously. Too much water is the chief cultivation error for this group of plants. Miltonias are particularly sensitive to water on their new growth, and this can very rapidly lead to rot setting in.

Dormancy

When the new growth has finished, the plant should be kept somewhat drier, though never allowed to dry out completely, though it may still be several weeks before there is a sign of the new flowering stem. If this develops before

▼ Miltonias are usually sold in container pots, but are best repotted into smaller pots.

Keep it in the family

Many orchid genera are closely related and it is therefore possible to cross not only species within one genus, but also to produce intergeneric hybrids. Thus _Miltonia (Miltoniopsis)_ are involved in many such crosses, with, for example, _Brassia, Oncidium, Ada_ and _Odontoglossum_. Most of these not only have fine flowers, but they are also easier to grow (see Intergeneric Hybrids, page 56). Above: _Brassada_ Mivada 'ROC', a _Brassia × Ada_ cross.

the pseudobulbs have become fully mature, which occasionally happens, you should continue to water the plant regularly.

Ventilation

Circulation of air will keep the most harmful pest away – red spider mite. However, there must never be so much movement in the air that the humidity drops below 30 per cent.

Feeding

The roots of miltonias are very sensitive to salt. Nevertheless, during the growing period

you should apply an orchid fertiliser at every third watering. But the dose should be reduced to about half the recommended amount. When watering, never pour liquid fertiliser directly on to the roots. Orchid experts cover the pot with a layer of sphagnum moss, which provides additional protection for the fine roots.

Repotting and compost

The best time for repotting miltonias is at the beginning of the growing period, preferably in autumn. If possible, avoid the summer, as the high temperatures put stress on the plant. When repotting, take care not to set the plant too deeply in the compost, and when watering make sure that water does not run on to the shoots, since this can quickly cause rotting to occur. Keep miltonias drier during this time. Only when new roots start to grow should regular watering be resumed. Miltonias prefer to be in small pots, so it is better to repot annually and ensure sufficient drainage. The compost should be relatively fine (Compost Type A if you are mixing it yourself, see page 24). Use only the finer parts of the compost by sieving out the coarser elements of the mixture. As is usual in the case of orchids that grow sympodially, the plant can be divided, but only after two new shoots have developed to the same height as the plant itself. At least three old pseudobulbs must remain on the new plant. As these rarely have their own healthy roots, it is recommended that the new plant is anchored in the pot by means of a stake or a hook.

◀ Too late to save this specimen, even though a new shoot has appeared. This orchid should have been repotted in a small pot to give the plant a better chance.

Expert tips

1 Buying

First of all look at the general condition of the plant and never buy one that is not firm. Avoid also plants with too many unopened buds – those on which only one-third of the flowers are already open will have the longest flowering period. And never buy plants that are growing together with others in a tray or pot.

2 The 'concertina' effect

Whether due to too much water, fertiliser or drought, miltonias and their relatives react rapidly with a malformation in the leaf, the so-called 'concertina' disease. In such cases, the development of the shoot is persistently disturbed, so that growth periodically comes to a standstill. Each new spurt of growth results in a fold in the shoot. This damage can only occur when there is a particular combination of light, temperature and air humidity, and it is usually irreparable if the roots are damaged. It is often a consequence of root

rot caused by overwatering or old plant compost. If this problem occurs the plant should be transferred immediately to a new pot with fresh compost.

3 My *Miltonia* will simply not flower!

This mostly happens when the shoots have not matured properly. Before the plant produces buds, a new shoot develops, each successive shoot being smaller than the previous one. The remedy is strict observance of the dormant period. Plants which produce strong shoots and yet do not flower should simply be kept in cooler conditions.

4 What to watch out for in the greenhouse

Miltonias do not do well in a greenhouse with many other species, as their requirements differ considerably from the usual division into 'temperate' or 'cold'. It is better to put them outside during the summer (see 5).

5 Is it possible to put miltonias outside in summer?

A spell outside from late spring until early autumn is highly recommended, as the most suitable temperatures occur then. The situation should be in partial shade, and direct sun must be avoided.

6 Growing epiphytically

Miltonias can in principle be grown epiphytically, but they will dry out even more quickly than in a pot. The most suitable are the natural forms, especially *Miltonia spectabilis* **6a** and comparable species. If the air is sufficiently humid in the greenhouse, conservatory or display case, clay

6b

6a

tubes **6b** can be successful. They transmit the dampness directly to the roots.

7 What happens after flowering?

Although this does not necessarily happen, miltonias and their hybrids with other genera are capable of producing a new shoot about every eight months together with a flowering stem. So on one and the same plant there may be a new shoot and also an inflorescence. Therefore you need to be sufficiently sensitive when watering to accommodate both types of development (rest and growth). Normally the flowering stems do not need to be supported, though plants are often sold staked for reasons of transport. Stems that have flowered should be promptly cut off, since the falling flowers can quickly cause rot on the sensitive leaves. The remaining stem is removed only when it is really dry. Either cut it off or carefully twist it until it breaks free from the pseudobulb. By the way, miltonias sometimes grow better on a windowsill than in a greenhouse.

7

8

8 Bud drop

Commonly, miltonias bear buds that do not develop into flowers. They either drop off or shrivel up. Unlike *Phalaenopsis* there is, unfortunately, no second chance of a new flowering stem. Apart from any common faults in cultivation, the cause is often entirely due to moving a plant from a greenhouse containing damp air to a room where the air is dry.

9 Pests and diseases*

Incorrect care ⑥ – ⑧ frequently results in the so-called 'concertina' effect. Many mistakes may be revealed on the relatively delicate, soft leaves: too much or too little light (see above) and too much salt, indicated by brown tips to the leaves and ultimately by brown leaf-veins. Brown root-tips and changes in the plant compost ① are a warning sign. Although scale insects and mealybugs may do some harm ㉘, the worst pests are red spider mites ㉜, followed by thrips ㉜ and whitefly ㉟. Fungal diseases and bacteria ⑥ – ⑧ as well as the increasingly common fungus gnats ⑤ can also cause problems.

10 Hydroculture

Miltonias and their hybrids with brassias can certainly be cultivated by this method, but it is definitely not for beginners. In hydroculture choose exclusively fine pellets, and only repot when the new growth becomes visible. The orchids should be kept in small pots, and only given liquid (not slow-release) fertilisers. The water level should range between minimum and optimum, never maximum. Do not water during the dormant period since the expanded clay pellets retain sufficient moisture.

*The numbers refer to the Appendix, page 135ff.

◄ In this case, the new shoot is showing signs of rot. The usual cause is water trapped within the shoot, but rotting can also result from cold, especially if the retail outlet is cold. Such a shoot cannot be saved. Cut it out, and dust the wound with fungicide.

◄ The wrinkled pseudobulb indicates damaged roots. Additionally, the flower stem has not emerged from the leaf axil and cannot be saved. The orchid is best replanted in a smaller pot.

Intergeneric hybrids

Intergeneric hybrids

Because of the close similarity of their flowers a new plant group has been introduced on to the market under the collective term Cambria. In fact, this term not only covers various varieties but even various genera. One name but many plants, so what exactly is the orchid I have bought? Nowadays the entire group is known by the name of one of these intergeneric hybrids, Cambria. It originally comes from South America, especially Brazil and Colombia. Cambrias include both bigeneric hybrids, whose names are made up from parts of their parents' names (e.g. *Miltonia* × *Brassia* = *Miltassia*, *Odontoglossum* × *Oncidium* = *Odontocidium*, or *Odontoglossum* × *Miltonia* = *Odontonia*), and intergeneric hybrids composed of at least three genera. These have been given a new name (e.g. *Odontoglossum* × *Cochlioda* × *Miltonia* = *Vuylstekeara*). So plants called vuylstekeara are really cambria. Most of the orchids now on sale for growing at home are intergeneric hybrids. Of these the best known are *Wilsonara* (= *Odontoglossum* × *Cochlioda* × *Oncidium*), *Colmanara* (= *Odontoglossum* × *Miltonia* × *Oncidium*) and *Beallara* (= *Brassia* × *Cochlioda* × *Miltonia* × *Oncidium*) as well as *Burrageara* (= *Cochlioda* × *Miltonia* × *Odontoglossum* × *Oncidium*). It may seem at first that the name is unimportant as long as you like the flower, but if you want to find out more about the plant you will need to know its correct name. An orchid nursery will provide the greatest opportunity for doing this, but you can also get help from the Internet.

For cultivation purposes the correct name is fortunately not so important, as the similarities outweigh the differences. Interbreeding has made

▼ This, an English cultivar from 1931, is the true ***Vuylstekeara* Cambria 'Plush'** that gave the hybrid group its name (Cambria).

► ***Vuylstekeara* Fall in Love**, a new generic cross from *V.* Mem. Mary Kavanaugh × *Odontioda* Helen Stead. The wealth of names reflects its complex origin.

▼ *Beallara* **Tahoma Glacier 'Green'**. This vigorous interhybrid flowers all year round and has very large flowers, up to 13 cm (5 in) across. It produces large plants in a short time, and may be propagated by division.

◄ This *Brassia*-hybrid shows little outward sign of that genus. But once a *Brassia*, always a *Brassia*, so it should be grown accordingly.

▼ *Odontonia* **Susan Bogdanow** (× *Odontonia* Avril Gay × *Miltonia* Franz Wichmann). Another easy hybrid, flowering at least twice a year.

▼ *Burrageara* **Nelly Isler** flowers all the year and has the flat flowers of *Miltonia*. A fantastic grower, it can also flower in two distinct flushes. The flower stalks do not always need support.

▶ **Odontocidium Hansueli Isler** (*Odontoglossum* Burkhard Holm × *Odontoglossum* Tiger Hambühren), a hybrid with the genus *Odontoglossum* twice in its parentage. Prefers slightly cooler conditions.

it possible to create from somewhat tricky parent plants progeny that are really easy to look after and make excellent houseplants. In addition, hybridisation has made available an indescribable range of colours and forms. So in choosing a plant, the orchid lovers can be guided by personal preference, without having to study beforehand the plant's cultivation requirements. Of course you can try growing individual species as well as the cultivated varieties, but an exact knowledge of their care will be necessary.

▶ **Odontoglossum Anna-Claire** (= O. *maculatum* × O. Geyser Gold). This has some of the charm of one of the most expensive of orchids, the 'Star of Colombia', *Odontoglossum crispum*.

▲ **Wilsonara Tiger Brew**. Parents: *Odontioda* Mem. Rudolph Pabst × *Odontocidium* Tiger Hambühren. Large flowers, good durability, sturdy growth. A vigorous plant such as this can benefit from plentiful feeding.

► *Oncidium* **Sweet Sugar**. The flowers resemble an insect, in a clever 'trick' of nature. In the wild, such plants use the insect's reproductive behaviour to guarantee their own continued survival.

Colmanara **Wildcat**, derived from *Odontonia* Rustic Bridge × *Odontocidium* Crowborough. Many varieties are available. The individual flower is remarkable, as is the effect of the multi-flowered inflorescence.

◄ *Odontoglossum* Rawdon Jester, a hybrid whose individual flowers resemble those of *Rossioglossum grande*, although the inflorescence is rather larger. Looks sensational on any windowsill. May be kept relatively cool.

Cultivation

▼ Essential equipment includes containers (pots, baskets, etc.), compost (moistened the previous day), sharp secateurs, binding material, sticks, and water. If the roots are healthy, remove only those that would be damaged or bent on repotting. Add the compost carefully after inserting the plant.

Temperature, light and humidity

They may have difficult names but they are easy to grow. They should stand in a fairly bright to half-shady place in normal room temperature, if possible not over 25°C (77°F) in summer, but always with a lower temperature at night. Generally they should be protected from direct sunlight.

With regard to air humidity, intergeneric hybrids have no particular requirements, but like all orchids prefer the humidity to be at least about 40 per cent. Trays to stand the pots on and the proximity of other plants is also important. Although there is no definite dormant period, you should only provide enough moisture after the plants have flowered to prevent the pseudo-bulbs from shrivelling. If possible, always combine the reduction in water with a lower tempera-ture. The end of the rest period is indicated by the appearance of a new shoot or shoots.

Watering

Keep the plant moderately damp, and immerse it from time to time, but afterwards merely spray it. Test with the finger before watering and use only lukewarm, lime-free water. Special care should be taken in the case of plants in com-posts consisting mainly of peat. Such plants should be repotted as soon as possible into a compost with a firm structure. Large, rather round pseudobulbs indicate a fairly long dormant period. Flat pseudobulbs, usually *Miltoniopsis*, may generally be kept damper, although they will also need a suitable rest period.

Ventilation

The whole group requires fresh air, consequently their surroundings should be well ventilated even in winter, but of course avoid cold air blowing directly on to the plants. And beware of frost!

Feeding

Plants in this group are sometimes very large indeed, and gardeners need not be mean with fertilisers, at least not in the ideal conditions of a greenhouse. But it is also important that a plant should be gradually acclimatised to room conditions when it is to be moved indoors. Even intergeneric hybrids should only be given fertiliser at every third watering during the growing period. However, immediately after buying you can safely apply an orchid fertiliser at least weekly to plants in flower. But after flowering has finished return to the normal amount. In general, these plants will tolerate a comparatively large amount of fertiliser.

Repotting and compost

With the appearance of new growth, not necessarily in winter, you can repot. The new pot should be big enough for two years' growth. When dividing the plant, return only four to seven pseudobulbs, using the rest to start a new plant. Even these pseudobulbs can be used for propagation purposes. If it has sufficient space do not divide the plant, since larger specimens produce more and larger flowers. Before putting the plant back, remove damaged and diseased roots. The shoots will determine the depth of the plant in the pot. When choosing the compost (Compost Type A if you are mixing it yourself, see page 24) ensure that it is not too fine and press it down firmly in the pot. The usual drainage is necessary. Plants without roots should be supported with a stake or a hook. They should never be loose in the compost or be planted too deeply. Use shallow pots – hanging pots are also suitable.

Other orchids in the group

• *Oncidium*: large genus with about 680 species. Most have yellow flowers, long flower stalks, or short inflorescences with small flowers.

• *Odontoglossum*: about 200 species. *Odontoglossum bictoniense* and hybrids are ideal houseplants.

• The closely related genus *Rossioglossum* contains the hybrid 'Walter Raleigh' which has impressive flowers, as well as the species *R. grande*. Both require a dormant period to induce flowering.

Expert tips

■ Buying

In the first place make sure that the pseudobulbs are firm and healthy, and look closely at the roots. The change of location will normally be tolerated quite well. Once again, one-third of the stem in flower guarantees the longest flowering time. Particularly in the case of the intergeneric hybrids you can often pick up a bargain, since plants which have already flowered are frequently offered for sale at half the original selling price. As long as the general condition of the plant is good there is no risk, for all the varieties quickly come into flower again. Because in this group the pollen cap that protects the pollen comes off easily, and the flower then fades early, you should only buy plants with undamaged flowers.

▪ Can I shorten long flowering stems?

In many of the intergeneric hybrids, especially the *Oncidium* hybrids, there are smaller but more numerous flowers on the stem, which then becomes extremely long. Anyone who thinks that it is enough to just pinch off the tip will find that side branches will soon develop. Smaller-flowered forms can be left to grow freely, but large-flowered varieties must be staked. Fairly thin bamboo canes can be used to support the flowering stem. In natural forms and hybrids of the first generation support is normally not needed. The best method is to use bast or binding wire and to fix it in at least two places.

▪ Bud drop

In addition to the well-known problems associated with moving the plants after purchase or incorrect conditions for cultivation or change of location, lack of light is usually to blame for bud drop. Flower development can slow down during the darker season of the year, or even come to a standstill. This is normal. After all, why should a plant flower if there are no insects about?

▪ When do the intergeneric hybrids flower?

This cannot be established with regard to a particular season of the year or even particular months, although the flowering period occurs mainly during the months with the most light. Well-grown specimens can develop one or even two flowering stems every eight months.

So there can be several shoots and also mature flowers at the same time. In the winter months, the period of development is distinctly longer that during the lighter time of the year.

5 My Cambria will simply not flower!

If the growth during the year is well developed then the cause is usually too much fertiliser or too much warmth without a reduction at night. The plant just feels too healthy! On the other hand, if the shoots produced during the year are inadequate, become ever smaller and look rather pathetic (with more than two to a pseudobulb), you can assume that there is root damage due to overwatering. Luckily it is possible to rescue an orchid in this state by repotting it in good time.

4

4

6 Growing epiphytically

They can certainly be mounted on bark, since all their ancestors are epiphytes. However there should be a longish period in which to accustom the plant to the change (see Fertilisers, page 61). Plants which are tied up do not appear ostentatious, which is more than can be said for many of the intergeneric hybrids available commercially.

7 **Is it possible to put the plants outside in summer?**

They can be stood outside in a shady place in summer or hung up, preferably in a deciduous tree – a conifer is less suitable. If there are long periods of rain, some protection from an excess of water will be necessary. Their greatest enemies outdoors are slugs and snails, and also ants.

8 **What to watch out for in the greenhouse**

Intergeneric hybrids are best suited to a temperate greenhouse, and they can be grown in pots or hanging baskets. As their cultivation is very simple, there should be no real difficulties. In fact in a greenhouse it is scale insects and mealybugs rather

than spider mites that are likely to cause problems. There must always be adequate ventilation, especially in summer, while in winter a ventilator is required to ensure there is movement in the air.

9 Can I make plant containers for orchids myself?

You can of course construct small baskets yourself out of wood, wire **9a** or plastic, but you can also use containers like the baskets sold for water plants **9b**, which will serve other purposes. So the shallow pots used for azaleas are better for orchids than the normal type of pot. It is, however, important that the container is not made of any materials that are likely to be harmful to the plants. For example, zinc can have a toxic effect when it is in contact with the salts in fertilisers, and of course in the case of wood, any wood preservatives should be avoided. Always ensure that the proportions are correct, so choose shallow rather than tall containers. The special orchid pots made of clay are very suitable as they have sufficiently large holes in them. But you can make these yourself on your next pottery course! Baskets made of larch wood are particularly resinous and therefore extremely durable.

9 a

10 Pests and diseases*

Easily avoidable errors in cultivation include too much water and the use of hard water. Mistakes recognisable in the compost ①–③ can also be avoided. You should keep an eye open for scale insects and mealybugs ㉘, ㉙ and also spider mites ㉝. Fungal diseases and bacteria ⑥–⑧ as well as fungus gnats ⑤ are a real danger. The best treatment consists of early recognition and prompt action. Virus attacks are fairly rare ㉚, and slugs and snails ㉟ are usually only a pest outdoors. Problems in bud development are almost always due to incorrect cultivation, and only rarely because of a change in location or after purchase.

11 Hydroculture

Intergeneric hybrids can certainly be grown by this method. But take care that they are moved at the right time and are allowed to have their dormant period. During this time the plants can occasionally be kept completely dry. Expanded clay pellets will maintain the degree of moisture necessary to keep them alive for at least two to three weeks. The use of fertilisers is the same as when the plants are growing in compost, but always use a liquid fertiliser.

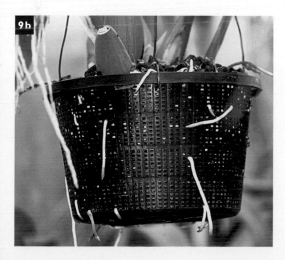

9 b

*The numbers refer to the Appendix, page 135ff.

Cattleya

Cattleya – a tropical beauty

In 1824 the Englishman William Cattley (hence the name of the genus) received a parcel of plants from South America, which were wrapped in long pieces of plant material that had been used as packaging. Today we know that these were in fact the pseudobulbs of *Cattleya labiata*, which at the time were grown out of mere curiosity and went on to produce spectacular flowers the following year! This first flower triggered an orchid trend throughout Europe, which persists to this day. There are some 30 species in this South and Central American genus, and it can easily be crossed with other genera. Such hybrids include for example: *Laeliocattleya* (= *Cattleya* × *Laelia*) and *Epicattleya* (= *Cattleya* × *Epidendrum*; see list on pages 28–29).

► **Brassocattleya Pastorale** shows the fringed lip of *Brassavola*. Some members of this genus are now called *Rhyncholaelia*, including the commonly crossed species *Brassavola* (*Rhyncholaelia*) *digbyana*. Typically fragrant.

◄ *Laeliocattleya* **Gold Digger**, an easy-growing, early-flowering mini-cattleya, almost always multi-flowered. It is hard to fail with this plant.

◄ *Laeliocattleya* **Thai Glow** has medium-sized, robust and long-lasting flowers. Requires bright, temperate, warm conditions. Grows easily and flowers reliably.

▲ *Otaara* **Hwa Yuan Bay** – a new intergeneric hybrid, this time from four genera – *Brassavola* × *Broughtonia* × *Cattleya* × *Laelia*. Rather complicated for such a pretty plant.

► *Brassocattleya* **Binosa 'Wabush Valley'** AM/AOS. The letters denote that this plant has received an award, in this case the Award of Merit of the American Orchid Society. Prefers a warm, bright position.

69

The genus *Cattleya* can be subdivided into two groups, which, however, have the same cultivation needs: 'single-leaved' and 'twin-leaved' (referring to the number of leaves on a single pseudobulb). *Cattleya labiata* and *Cattleya mossiae* have particularly large flowers (up to 17 cm/7 in across!) and there are also small- and multi-flowered species. In most cases the plants grow quite tall, *Cattleya guttata* to at least 150 cm (5 ft), with the flower stalk adding up to another 30 cm (1 ft). Unfortunately, the large-flowered *Cattleya* do not keep for long. Thus the trend has been to strive towards creating hybrids of single-flowered genera with longer-lasting flowers. In principle, cattleyas are easy to cultivate, even though they are not particularly fond of warm rooms. Crossing with other genera and warm-growing species, however, has created suitable houseplants.

▶ *Sophrolaeliocattl eya* **Mahalo Jack**. The parent species *Cattleya walkeriana* from Brazil is visible in this hybrid. This relatively small plant has quite large flowers.

▶ *Epicattleya* **Plicboa** has the typical flower shape and long stalk of *Epidendrum*. Robust, flowers reliably, and tolerates full light.

▲ *Sophrolaeliocattleya* **Mae Hawkins** has fiery red, medium-sized flowers. Best grown in a hanging basket as the abundant flowers hang downwards and thus need no extra support.

◄ *Epilaeliocattleya* **Don Herman**, a cross between *Laeliocattleya* Gold Digger and *Epidendrum stanfordianum*. Another hybrid involving *Epidendrum*, but whose influence is seen here only in the shape of the lip.

◄ *Potinara* **Burana Beauty**. The splendid flowers are attractive enough on their own, but combined with their lemon fragrance make this a real gem of an orchid.

► *Brassolaeliocattleya* **Golden Mul** has relatively small flowers. They are, however, long-lasting and of an impressively intense colour. It also tolerates more light than other cattleyas.

Cultivation

Temperature, light and humidity

Cattleyas love being in slight shade or low light. They can also adapt to bright sunshine as long as they are gradually introduced to it. Despite their almost succulent leaves, they can easily burn when exposed to strong light and warmth, especially under glass. Cattleyas enjoy room temperature during the day and a distinct reduction in temperature at night (of at least 5°C/9°F). They need exposure to constant air movement, but not especially high relative humidity (about 40 per cent is ideal). Even though they do not need to be sprayed as often as say *Phalaenopsis*, it is nevertheless necessary to do so indoors in the summer or if the air is dry. Since *Cattleya* needs a period of dormancy to flower, it is essential to allow this at the end of the growing period.

Watering

Allow the growing medium to dry out completely between waterings (if possible use rainwater or lime-free water). Then water plentifully, and wait again. In the rest period this could last up to two or three weeks. Surplus water must be removed from the saucer under the pot.

Ventilation

Cattleyas need a lot of fresh air, because in many of their natural habitats they grow at a great height in the treetops. You must also make sure they have plenty of fresh air during the dormant period. On they other hand, they are not very sensitive to draughts, as long as they are not too cold.

Feeding

Being epiphytes or lithophytes, these plants are adapted to conditions of low nutrient supply, but due to their large size and abundant flowering, they usually need feeding. But it is worth remembering that they generally do better with less rather than too much fertiliser. What matters is the state of the individual plant. Periods of rest and growth cycles are just as important as light and water quality. Healthy plants should be fed when the new shoots appear. If you do not want to use a regular orchid fertiliser, you can mix your own. At the onset of growth

▼ Cattleyas are always the central attraction at orchid exhibitions and displays, and they have become the symbol of tropical orchids. However, they have a relatively short flowering period.

1 **2** **3** **4** **5**

use N:P:K in the proportion 3:2:2 plus trace nutrients. During growth the proportion of N:P:K should be 2:3:3 plus trace nutrients. Always adapt the frequency and amount of dose to the growth of the plant. If the concentration is too high it can lead to root damage, or arrested growth of any new shoots, which can blacken and die (there are of course other possible causes for this).

Repotting and compost

If necessary you can repot when new shoots appear. Before the new shoots are formed, new roots are clearly visible. The root layer indicates the right height for the plant in the pot. Before you place the plant in the new pot, remove all rotten, brown and wet roots. Since there needs to be room for at least two new shoots in the pot, quite large pots are needed as some cattleyas have long rhizomes. For this reason, shallow pots or baskets are suitable: then the amount of compost is reduced and the plants are able to dry out more easily. Cattleyas to be separated must have at least eight pseudobulbs and two new leading shoots. For those without roots, the last shoot must be supported with a cane or hook as a replacement root (see pictures **1** – **4**). Try to not move the pot until the roots are firmly anchored in the growing medium.

Propagation is easy using *backbulbs*. However, you should remove any loose tissue from the pseudobulbs, or at least check it as pests often hide there. Cattleyas need very coarse compost (see how to mix your own compost type A on page 24). In the case of ready mixed compost, choose the coarser grades. The compost must retain a stable structure, and it is important to use only high-quality compost. A high proportion of bark will improve the structure at first, but only for one season. Coconut chippings are better, as these are more stable.

6

▲ Cattleyas can be propagated easily using backbulbs. Here a length of wire is being used as a root substitute. After about three months a new shoot develops under the plastic (**6** and below left). Then remove the plastic and plant as normal in compost after root development.

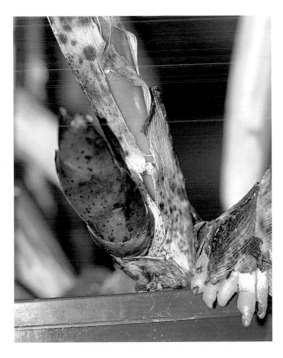

◄ New roots develop at the same time as the fresh shoot (right).

Expert tips

1 Buying

Since cattleyas grow very slowly and do not normally flower until they are five or more years old, they are very expensive compared with say *Phalaenopsis*. For this reason, it is important when purchasing to make sure the plant is in good overall condition. It is best to buy either a plant

with 'small' buds or one in full bloom. Flowers which have only just begun to open often do not survive the stress of transport very well. Because of the age of the plant, it is normal for leaf/petal or bulb damage and dry spots, etc. to be present. Old shoots are also likely to shrink. The main thing is that the newest two shoots are perfect.

Watch out for pests, especially under the fibrous layer of the bulb (**1a**). Do not buy a plant with ragged or misshapen leaves, or with longitudinal dotted lines on the leaves, which can indicate a virus.

2 **When do cattleyas flower?**

Depending on the parentage, cattleyas can flower in the middle of the dormant period without forming a new shoot. Flowers are built with the new shoots following the end of the annual growth cycle, and also at all other times. This flexibility has resulted from their dependence in the wild on pollinating insects. Cattleyas are an exception to the rule – normally orchids first form a shoot and then flower. Such exceptions can also be found in other genera.

3 **Lack of flowers**

The most frequent cause for this is immaturity of the shoot. The new shoot must be at least as large as its predecessor. Always ensure a dormant period.

NOTE **Freeing the flowers**

The flower buds are protected by a sheath that in time can completely dry out. This is normal as long as the bud itself stays green. If you hold it up to the light, you can usually see the bud inside. Unfortunately, indoors the sheath may become hard, and sometimes the bud can even become trapped. In this case it is important to cut open the sheath, taking care not to damage the bud.

8

4 **Bud drop**

In addition to arrested development (see above), buds can also be aborted. The reasons are usually due to avoidable mistakes in cultivation, mostly smoke (or ethylene) and cold draughts.

5 **Can cattleyas be kept with other houseplants?**

Cattleyas prefer to be kept in a group, especially with other sun-loving plants such as cacti and succulents.

6 **Is it possible to put cattleyas outside in summer?**

If the plant is protected from the rain, it can be kept in the garden during the summer. However at temperatures below 12°C (54°F) it should be brought back inside the house. If it is outside, watch out for ants, slugs and snails, which are especially partial to the soft buds and flowers. In the wild, cattleyas often protect themselves with ants. Before they flower, sugary drops form on the bud, as a 'reward' for the ants for keeping guard. In cultivation – without ants – mould can develop on these drops. However, in the long run this does not damage flower development.

7 **Should cattleya flowers be supported?**

Tying up the plant or supporting the flower is really only necessary with large-flowered varieties, or those with more than three flowers. Sometimes it is a good idea to raise the inflorescence above the leaves to be able to admire the flowers better.

8 **Growing epiphytically**

In fact, cattleyas can be grown successfully epiphytically, as long as the relative humidity is not less than 50 per cent. The plant should be tied when the new shoot has been formed, and it must be tied very tightly, with only a small amount of substrate underneath.

9 What to watch out for in the greenhouse

Cattleyas are some of the most impressive greenhouse orchids, and need light and airy conditions. When the greenhouse is not being aired, a constant fan is required. In an array of plants from different genera, cattleyas should be placed in the brightest spots – at best tied to bark or in a decorative wooden basket. They should only be shaded from late spring to the end of summer. The humidity in the greenhouse needs be high only in the growing period.

10 Pests and diseases*

An accumulation of salt content in the compost, perhaps from hard water, over-fertilising and/or waterlogging leads to root damage, loss of the new shoots or in extreme cases to loss of the entire plant ①–③. Fungi and bacteria play a big part in these cases, of course ⑥–⑧. Mealybugs and scale insects can reproduce and spread, notably on the fibrous layer of the bulb and on the flower sheath. Constant checking is therefore important. Viruses are also possible ㊱ 10a . Only an expert can be certain, but if you suspect a problem, the plant should be isolated immediately.

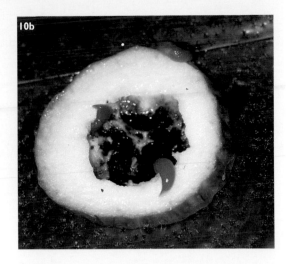

10b

Always work with disinfected tools. Snails and slugs are attracted to the delicate flowers outdoors and in the greenhouse. A dry strip of cotton wool can be laid around the inflorescences of cattleyas, or pieces of cucumber to keep the molluscs away. *Botrytis* ㉕ can become a problem if there is high humidity during autumn and winter.

11 Hydroponics

Cattleyas, as lithophytes, are well suited to hydroculture, as long as they are treated in the same way as if they were growing in compost. As well as respecting the dormant periods, watering frequency should be adapted to the substrate. In a hydroculture system, after filling up to 'optimum', let the plant dry out completely until the new shoot appears.

10a

*The numbers refer to the Appendix, page 135ff.

Cymbidium

Cymbidium – the tough ones

The cymbidiums that are usually available commercially are really too large to be maintained as indoor plants, but because of their imposing flower stems they are still frequently bought. However, things do not always turn out all right even with a new flower stem. Smaller or small-flowered varieties are increasing in popularity, since they are not only more suitable for a room, but they also flower again more readily. Originally, large-flowered varieties were only cultivated as cut flowers.

Their most important ancestors come from Burma, Thailand, India, Nepal, Vietnam, Indonesia and Australia, where they grow at different heights and temperatures as epiphytes, or more rarely on the ground. From time immemorial the Chinese have known and prized them as tub-plants, and grown in this way they could again make their mark. Cymbidiums first came to notice because of their long-lasting flowers, which will delight the eye for several weeks even when cut. An additional contribution to their success lies in the fact that some of the principal parent-species (*Cymbidium lowianum* and *Cymbidium giganteum*) flower in spring. As their importance as cut flowers declined, gardeners with an eye for business made cymbidiums into pot-orchids, unfortunately not always to the lasting joy of the purchaser.

▲ *Cymbidium* × **Big Trees** is still a little like its green-flowered ancestors, such as *Cymbidium lowianum*, first found in Burma in 1877. It is very popular for cut flowers.

▶ *Cymbidium* × **Nicole's Valentine** is one of the miniature cymbidiums, referring to the flower size – the plant itself grows quite large. It is impressively multi-flowered.

► *Cymbidium* × **Gymer 'Cooksbridge'** is a typical cut flower orchid with many brightly coloured, long-lasting flowers, especially when left on the plant. It still requires optimal growing conditions.

◄ Pale orchids are easily damaged. All large-flowered varieties need staking, but these need special care. The pollen caps are very loose so pollination occurs easily, shortening the life of the flowers.

◄ A mixture of open and cupped flower shapes and large- and small-flowered varieties. Cymbidiums offer an even wider range of colours and shapes. The open, mainly older varieties often seem more elegant and less 'artificial'.

Cultivation

Temperature, light and humidity

Cymbidiums are hungry for light, but do not tolerate direct sun during the summer. In summer they prefer day temperatures to be about 30°C (86°F), while at night the thermometer can gently sink to 15°C (59°F). In autumn and winter, temperatures of 15–18°C (59–64°F) by day and 8–10°C (46–50°F) at night are ideal, although these figures naturally depend on the growth-cycle of the particular variety concerned. In any case, mature plants need a considerable difference in day and night temperatures, and indoors that is normally not possible to arrange. In addition, there should be 60–80 per cent humidity, which is also difficult to achieve in a room.

Some miniature cymbidiums depart from the above conditions, but unfortunately it is difficult to know which these are. There are in fact large-leaved plants with small flowers which are cultivated like the big ones, even if they are somewhat more tolerant of the temperature. The genuine 'minis', both in size of plants and flowers, are really attractive and make rewarding pot-orchids. They develop arching inflorescences which should never be tied up, for only in this way do they exhibit their full beauty. As their ancestors are at home in warm regions of the tropics, they are best indoors, with an average daytime temperature of 20°C (68°F) and not lower than 17°C (63°F) at night. They can equally well be cultivated alongside moth orchids.

Watering

Whatever grows quickly needs abundant water and nutrients. During the growing period therefore there should be copious watering, but even at other times the compost must never be allowed to dry out completely. Unlike other orchids, cymbidiums have no dormant period, and new shoots appear at the same time as the flowers. But it is important that the pseudobulbs and shoots mature properly. In spite of a lower temperature at night, if the pseudobulbs are not mature there will be no flowers. The varieties that prefer warm conditions are particularly adaptable.

Ventilation

The genus requires plenty of fresh air, and the humidity of the air must not be too low. If the plant is outside it should be misted in the mornings to simulate dew formation. The varieties that

▼ Cymbidiums are 'hungry' orchids, so rather frequent feeding is imperative. Always use a regular orchid fertiliser.

like warm conditions should remain inside, but receive plenty of ventilation in summer.

Feeding

Cymbidiums, at least the large-flowered varieties, undoubtedly belong to the group of orchids that need abundant nutrients, and sometimes even the use of stronger kinds is recommended. You should not go to those lengths, although a fertiliser should be used at every second watering, or on every occasion if the dose is correspondingly reduced. It is best to select an orchid fertiliser with high nitrogen content. For eight weeks after mid-summer, use

an ordinary flower fertiliser, at least halving the dose, after which continue to apply fertiliser in the normal way. The fertiliser should be used throughout the year.

Repotting and compost

Cymbidiums like to fill their pots. Repotting is required only when the new shoot grows out over the edge of the pot or the pot splits because of the mass of roots. This can take a good two years. But after this time it will no longer be sufficient merely to remove some of the old compost, put the plant in a new pot and add new compost. A more drastic procedure must be adopted. In addition to secateurs a small hatchet may be required to open up the dense mass of roots. Large plants will demand effort and patience for you should, of course, disturb the roots as little as possible. When repotting, pseudobulbs without leaves can be removed, and

large plants divided up. Naturally, large plants come into flower more easily and produce more flowers. Five pseudobulbs per pot is the minimum. The pot itself should be as deep as possible (containers used in tree nurseries are very suitable) in order to provide space for at least two more years' growth. A mixture containing up to 20 per cent expanded clay pellets will give the compost a stable structure. For drainage, expanded clay pellets are better than expanded polystyrene. You can use any ready-made orchid compost as the base material (or mix Compost Type C yourself, see page 24).

Genuine mini-cymbidiums can be put in ordinary orchid compost in shallow or in hanging pots (Compost Type A if you are mixing it yourself, see page 24) for they are true epiphytes. Propagation from backbulbs is very easy, but if they have leaves remove them or at least shorten them first.

▲ You can be fairly rough when repotting cymbidiums and you may need a knife to open up the tight root ball. Important: use a firm orchid compost that retains moisture well.

Expert tips

1 Buying

In addition to general condition, which in the case of cymbidiums is usually very good, you should take account of the remarks above in connection with the early-flowering varieties. Do not buy any plants with root damage, or any that are loose in the pot or have brown and squashy roots. Also avoid plants whose roots are welling up over the edge of the pot **1b** or are lifting the plant upwards (it may mean that you will have to repot the plant immediately). Flowers that have already faded or have been damaged in transit can be easily recognised by the dark-coloured lip **1a** . Do not buy these!

2 My *Cymbidium* will simply not flower!

The answer to this, probably the most frequently asked question, is usually quite simple – because it is being kept too warm. Or, if it has been put out in the garden, because it has been brought in again at the start of summer. In the living room, it is missing the necessary drop in temperature at night. Consequently it must be placed in a greenhouse or conservatory, or in a light, cool hall, basement or shed, in the same way as tub-plants such as fuchsias are treated. When buds begin to appear, the *Cymbidium* should remain in its cool situation until it is in full flower, and only then should it be brought into the warm living room, otherwise there is a danger that the buds will drop off. If you cannot provide these conditions it is better to give up! New growth **2a** can easily be confused with flowering shoots **2b** . Note also that a rainy summer can also result in a year without flowers.

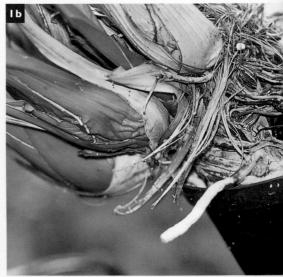

2a

2b

3 The new pseudobulb is much smaller

It is a bad sign in orchids when the new pseudobulb is smaller than its predecessor. However, in the case of cymbidiums it cannot be avoided, at least during the first year after it has been acquired, for the plants on sale are often no more than varieties grown for cut flowers that have been divided up or discarded. It is easy to check if the previous pseudobulb is considerably bigger than the one currently flowering. Sometimes large varieties that have been planted outside and used to produce cut flowers have been turned into pot-plants. The strength to produce the inflorescence comes from the best possible greenhouse cultivation, but in a room or a conservatory the strong fertilisers and also the carbon dioxide treatment given by the professionals will be lacking, so they will return to normal size. A small pseudobulb is no real reason for anxiety, but if this occurs repeatedly year after year, then it is due to incorrect care.

4 Bud drop

After the buds have appeared, the *Cymbidium* should not stand where it is too warm or where there are sharp fluctuations in temperature, otherwise the buds may not continue to develop and can ultimately fall off. Transport of the plant, too cold a temperature in the shop, and the use of plastic wrapping may also be possible causes to be taken into consideration.

5 Should I keep cymbidiums with other indoor plants?

They are really too large to stand on a windowsill. Instead they are more suitable for growing in a temperate to cool conservatory or as a tub-plant.

6 What to watch out for in the greenhouse

As far as temperature is concerned, cymbidiums belong in a temperate greenhouse, but they do like to have colder

8

8a

7

conditions at night. If you combine the stay in the greenhouse with a period outside throughout the summer, you will certainly be successful. The important requirements are high humidity, a light situation and good ventilation. The plants need to receive sufficient light, and therefore should not stand too close together. Make sure they are protected against slugs and snails, and check regularly for spider mites (see under Pests).

7 Varieties of *Cymbidium*

If you really want to grow cymbidiums it is necessary to make the right choice, and the range includes the miniature forms (see picture), which are free from problems. Choose only the early-flowering varieties, i.e. those that come into flower in autumn–winter. In this case, the onset of flower production occurs about three months before flowering, and therefore at a time of the year when you can easily keep the plants outside in temperatures that are naturally higher by day and lower at night. With varieties that flower from late winter to spring, keeping them in a room may inhibit the process of flower production. But if you put them in a conservatory or greenhouse there is a chance of success.

8 **Is it possible to put the plants outside in summer?**

It is not only possible, but an absolute necessity. A light situation should be chosen, even one in full sun if the plants have been carefully acclimatised. It is important that the humidity is as high as possible, if necessary by creating 'artificial dew' in the mornings by using a fine spray. They should, however ,be protected from too much rain or sun. Their stay outdoors can be extended until early autumn, but be sure to bring them indoors in good time before any frost, otherwise it may result in irreparable damage to the plants **8a** . For early-flowering varieties, if there are signs that flower buds are developing, the plants should be moved in good time to the place where they are to flower. The earlier this is done, the more likely are the flowers to continue to develop.

9 **Growing epiphytically**

For the large-flowered varieties, which may be partly epiphytic in origin, this may be appropriate, depending on their size. But in the case of some of the species and the miniature hybrids it is certainly suitable, and

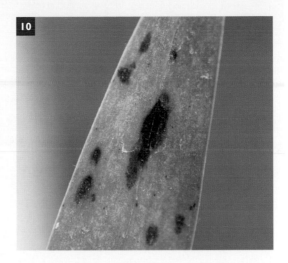

this technique displays the full beauty of the hanging flower stems. Most, for example *Cymbidium suave*, quickly grow aerial roots into the substrate.

10 **Pests and diseases***

Two pests are particularly prevalent on *Cymbidium* – scale insects ㉘, which hide among the leaves and between the scales covering the bulb, and spider mites ㉝, ⑮. Regular checks on the plants will avoid the worst damage ⑪, ⑮. Less frequently, there may be attacks by bacteria and moulds ⑦, ⑧, and sometimes even the roots are affected ⑥. Quite often there can be a problem with viruses ㊱, which may be difficult to recognise, or with an insufficiency or excess of nutrients ⑰, ⑱.

11 **Hydroculture**

The genus is well suited to this method of cultivation. But there is no great advantage, since watering cymbidiums is not a problem, indeed they can suffer from excess water. Switching to hydroculture is possible when growth starts, and because of the thick roots repeated rinsing is advisable after about three months.

*The numbers refer to the Appendix, page 135ff.

Paphiopedilum

Paphiopedilum – the slipper orchids

The slipper orchid (*Cypripedium*) is a well-known classic, and this genus and *Paphiopedilum* became popular well before the moth orchids. *Cypripedium* is a scarce orchid in the wild in Europe – and one of Britain's rarest flowers. The slipper orchids grown as houseplants are mainly from Asia and are superficially similar. *Paphiopedilum* is also a terrestrial orchid in the wild, but needs a humus-rich, loose growing medium, rather than normal compost.

▲ Not all slipper orchids are tropical. The flowers of the European **Cypripedium calceolus** also have the typical slipper shape, and there are also garden varieties of this genus.

► Small-flowered forms, such as this mature **Paphiopedilum** hybrid, often have more flowers than those with larger flowers.

▼ *Paphiopedilum* Maudiae has attractive marbled leaves, impressive even when not flowering.

▲ *Paphiopedilum* **Ashburtoniae** was produced in England in 1871 by Lady Ashburton. The earlier crosses had an open flower, and a more rounded form was developed later.

► Large-flowered forms are now often available, not just as cut flowers, but are often sold without the correct name, simply referred to as *Paphiopedilum* hybrids. They need patience as the flowers take a long time to develop, but are long-lasting.

► *Paphiopedilum* **Deperle** (= *Paphiopedilum delenatii* × *Paphiopedilum primulinum*) was raised in Paris in 1980 by M. Lecoufle. Unfortunately this variety is no longer commonly available.

Slipper orchids have no aerial roots and no velamen (or this is only temporary), but they develop root hairs, which increase the surface area of the roots considerably – a good adaptation to the loose growing medium.

The genus *Paphiopedilum*, which has given rise to many houseplants, is closely related to *Cypripedium*, *Phragmipedium* and *Selenipedium*, and all have slipper-like flowers. *Paphiopedilum* is restricted to tropical Asia (including Nepal, India, China, Vietnam, Laos, Indonesia and the Philippines). *Cypripedium*, sometimes grown in gardens, is from Europe, Asia, and the Americas, while *Selenipedium* and *Phragmipedium* are from South America. The latter is increasingly popular as a houseplant, especially *Phragmipedium besseae* with its red flowers. Red slipper orchids are no longer that unusual.

▼ Another selection from the hybrid *Paphiopedilum delenatii* × *Paphiopedilum primulinum*. It also has attractive, dark green marbled foliage.

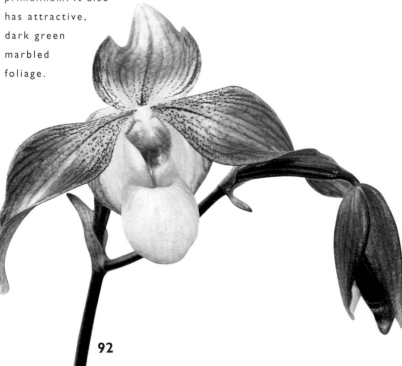

▼ *Paphiopedilum haynaldianum* var. **album** is a rarity not often seen. It is native to the Philippine island of Luzon.

◀ This hybrid of **Paphiopedilum glaucophyllum** is multi-flowered, but with somewhat smaller flowers. Unlike those of many hybrids, the flowers all open simultaneously.

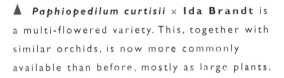

▲ **Paphiopedilum curtisii** × **Ida Brandt** is a multi-flowered variety. This, together with similar orchids, is now more commonly available than before, mostly as large plants.

◀ **Paphiopedilum Lebaudyanum** (= *Paphiopedilum haynaldianum* × *P. philippinense*). This variety can produce flowering stems to 100 cm (39 in) long – quite a sensation in any orchid collection.

▼ An unusual colour form. Orchids are now available in almost any colour.

Cultivation

Temperature, light and humidity

(The following suggestions only apply to *Paphiopedilum*.) The widespread view that slipper orchids with marbled leaves like warm sites and those with pure green, usually narrow leaves should be kept cooler is a good general rule but does not always apply to hybrids.

Marbled-leaf forms and hybrids do indeed prefer warm conditions – in summer 20–25°C (68–77°F), winter 17–22°C (63–72°F). Those with pure green foliage and narrow leaves prefer it slightly cooler – in summer by day 20–22°C (68–72°F), night 17–19°C (63–66°F), and in winter by day 18–20°C (64–68°F), night 13–16°C (55–61°F). Lowering the temperature after the main growing period is important for flower development.

Many-flowered species require warm-temperate conditions: summer 20–23°C (68–73°F), winter 18–22°C (64–72°F). This includes most of the many-flowered varieties with broad green leaves. These are well suited to normal indoor conditions and are comfortable at summer temperatures of 18–25°C (64–77°F), winter 16–20°C (61–68°F).

They also differ in light requirement. Many-flowered types and those with spotted foliage prefer bright light, but not direct sun, those with green foliage indirect light (e.g. a window that receives no direct sun). All species need high humidity, which indoors requires water trays. Humidity should not drop below 50 per cent.

Dormancy

In the case of slipper orchids requiring warm conditions, a dormant period is needed for flower development, and this is induced by lowering the temperature, especially at night, after the main growing phase. The others show no dormant phase.

Watering

The recipe for success is simple. Water regularly, but correctly, so that the compost always dries out in between waterings, but is not left dry for long periods. Be careful not to over-water, especially in the cooler season, as slipper orchids are easily attacked by fungi if they are waterlogged. Do not allow water to collect in the leaf axils – spraying is only necessary on very warm days when the humidity is low. Flush out the pot regularly to avoid salt accumulation.

Ventilation

Good ventilation is the best way to prevent problems with bacteria and fungi, which can arise with high humidity. But orchids should always be protected from cold air, especially near open windows.

► The fresh growth shows clearly in the centre of this relatively small slipper orchid. It is this shoot that will be flower-bearing.

NOTE A rather unusual slipper orchid

Phragmipedium Don Wimber
(= *Phragmipedium* Eric Young × *P. besseae*)
has ancestors in Central and South
America. These are mostly large plants
with long-lasting flowers. Flowering lasts
three to four months, sometimes as long as
11 months, with individual flowers opening
in succession. These are terrestrial orchids
living in a very moist, airy environment. In
cultivation they need temperate to fairly
warm conditions – 16–28°C (61–82°F) by
day, falling to 15–20°C (59–68°F) at night.
However *Phragmipedium besseae* and its
hybrids cannot tolerate too high
temperatures and are thus suitable for
windows that never receive direct sun. This
particularly fine species has conspicuous
deep red velvety flowers (an unusual colour
for a slipper orchid). The progeny are
particularly easy to cultivate. Compost
should never be allowed to dry out, and the
humidity should remain high, ideally
around 60–80 per cent – spray the
undersides of the leaves and the compost
surface several times a day. With no
dormant period, they should be fed
throughout the year, using an orchid
fertiliser at every third watering. Watch
out for fungi ⑥–⑧ and scale insects ㉘
(see page 135).

Feeding

Instructions for feeding slipper orchids range
from 'never' to 'at every watering'. Slipper
orchids are very sensitive to salt deposits in
the compost, especially when dry. Such salts
can damage the root hairs. Yet they do need
feeding. Some nourishment comes from the
compost, organic materials such as beech
leaves and bark yielding some nutrients.
It also depends on whether the orchid is a
small species or a large hybrid. Large- or
many-flowered orchids cannot be grown
without feeding. A good rule is to add
fertiliser at every third watering. For
hybrids, follow the instructions given
with the plant when purchased, but
reduce the dose by half for species and
small plants.

Repotting and compost

Slipper orchids can be propagated
vegetatively, but not by dividing. This happens
when they naturally fall apart, with no tearing,
cutting or breaking. It is important not to
miss the correct time, as *Paphiopedilum* only
put out new roots once during the growing
season, along with new shoots. It is vital to
provide adequate drainage at the base of the
pot. Slipper orchids need a fine compost
(sieving may be necessary), and this can be
mixed with half-rotted beech leaves and
sphagnum moss (such as is sold for hanging
baskets). Or you can create a mixture such
as type C (see page 24).
Old plant remains should first be removed
from the compost and unhealthy, soft or
mouldy roots cut off cleanly. Shallow
plastic pots are suitable, especially those
with good drainage, and the container
should not be too large. Place the plant
in the centre of the pot and do not compact
the compost, adding moss to the surface.
Do not feed for the first five weeks after
repotting.

Expert tips

1 Buying

Do not buy any plant with limp, short
leaves, or if it has a damp, thickened
surface, which can indicate unhealthy
roots. If the individual flower feels firm
then you can expect it to keep flowering.
Plants with buds generally tolerate
replanting rather well. Only choose plants
with several shoots – a single flowering
stem and an old shoot do not augur well for
future flowering.

2 Lack of flowers

This could be caused by wrong treatment,
such as over-watering, or often by keeping
it at the wrong temperature. Some

Paphiopedilum species and hybrids do
not like to be kept too warm. Also note
that the large-flowered and multi-flowered
hybrids have a long development period
and only flower a couple of times in three
years. Some outlets offer plants that
(like *Cymbidium*) are used in the cut flower
industry, and these have often been
grown in very large containers.
After division, such plants are
often very slow to grow and
flower (sometimes taking
more than a year) and need
a lot of patience.

3 Orchids outdoors

Only the green, narrow-leaved orchids can be put outside – in summer – and this encourages flowering. They do, however, need protection from direct sun and heavy rain.

4 Arrested flowering

If slipper orchids get too wet, the flower buds do not develop, and that year's flowers can be lost. This can only be remedied through correct watering.

5 Can slipper orchids be kept with other houseplants?

Slipper orchids can mix well with other leafy houseplants, especially where these can give the orchids some welcome shade. Those with large

4

soft leaves, e.g. begonias, help to maintain the humidity.

6 What to watch out for in the greenhouse

'Green fingers' are needed when growing slipper orchids. You also need the right greenhouse for the *Paphiopedilum* group in question – that is, a warm or temperate house – and also be aware that *Paphiopedilum*, especially the pure species, needs particular conditions, different from those of other orchids. Hybrids are another matter. High humidity and correct lighting are needed, along with a suitable watering regime – not too much, and place the plants on a grating so that they never get too cold or too wet at the roots.

7 Growing epiphytically

They are not suitable for growing epiphytically as almost all the species are terrestrial, although attractive pots can be used.

6

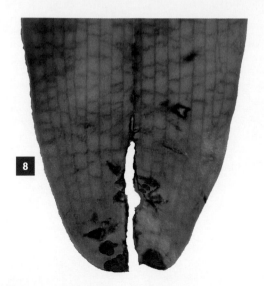

8 **One leaf says more than many words**
Pale, yellow-green or crinkled, dry leaves
are mostly the result of too much light.
Yellowing of older leaves may be caused
by lack of nitrogen, root damage or too low

a temperature. Reddish leaves (except
in the case of marbled varieties)
are also caused by too much light
(always shade).

9 **Symptoms**
Salt accumulation or too low a pH value
(see below) results in a characteristic
pale/dark brown pattern on the leaf tips.
Some varieties show these symptoms
even though they may otherwise grow
and flower normally. Too little or too
much water can cause the leaf tips of
slipper orchids to die back.

10 **Calcium**
Slipper orchid compost (especially for
the white varieties) should have regular
additions of lime, ideally at least every
12 weeks. It is best to use shell lime or

calcium carbonate, to deliver a slow dose. One teaspoon of lime is sufficient for a 12 cm (5 in) pot. If the water is hard, then there is no need to provide this extra calcium.

11 Pests and diseases*

Some diseases are easy to spot on the plants themselves – for example ①–③. Then there are springtails ④ and fungus gnats ⑤, which are an increasing problem of houseplants. However, the most serious are fungal and bacterial diseases ⑥–⑧. Root rot in *Paphiopedilum* can also be caused by a pot that is too large, by bad drainage, and by over-watering or watering at the wrong time. This can be avoided by letting the pots dry completely after watering. In the greenhouse, slugs and snails ㉚ can be another problem. Virus diseases ㊱ are rather uncommon. Spider mites ⑮, ㉝ can attack if the humidity is too low. Mealybugs and scale insects ㉙, ㉘ like to secrete themselves in the leaf axils, and should be checked for regularly. Occasionally, soft-skinned mites ㉞ are found on the buds, in which case an expert should be consulted.

12 Hydroponics

Like moth orchids, slipper orchids are suitable for hydroponic culture, and their terrestrial habit makes them good candidates for this technique. Slipper orchids lose their typical root hairs in hydro-cultivation, so transferring the plants can be tricky. Therefore only strongly growing plants with fresh shoots should be moved. Wash thoroughly before planting in the expanded clay pellets (or other hydroponic medium) to remove the fine dust and deposits. For *Paphiopedilum* the compost can be completely removed and the orchid planted in a pure hydroponic

medium. Once transplanted, they are usually very successful. Never let the water level indicator go above 'optimal' and always allow the system to dry out gradually. The clay pellets always retain enough moisture for a few days. Never allow water to accumulate.

---

* Numbers refer to those on pages 135ff.

12

Dendrobium

Dendrobium –
the tree-dwellers

▼ An attractive arrangement of **Dendrobium phalaenopsis-hybrids**. Such beautiful flowers are, however, very unsuited to cultivation.

Dendrobium is a very large genus possibly consisting of 1600 species, of which most are epiphytes, although a few are also lithophytes. They are to be found in a number of countries ranging from India to China, south-east Asia and Indonesia, as well as Australia and New Zealand. They range from small species which have only tiny pseudobulbs to others with pseudobulbs one metre (one yard) long. As they are found over such a large area, they naturally also come from different climate zones. However, only a few types are widely available. Orchid nurseries offer a larger selection. Flowering stems are almost always many-flowered and only rarely single-flowered.

Dendrobium thyrsiflorum

Most orchid books include *Dendrobium thyrsiflorum*, a species which resembles scrambled eggs in appearance but is only rarely available commercially. It grows in a monsoon climate in Burma and Northern Thailand, where there are three distinct seasons: cool (four or five months), hot (about four months, with peak temperatures around 40°C/104°F) and rainy (about four months), which overlaps with the hot season. About four-fifths of the annual rainfall comes in the rainy season. A high temperature is needed during the growing period, while in winter the plant prefers it sunny, cool (up to 12°C/54°F) and dry. It is only when the plant buds in late winter that more warmth should be slowly introduced. During the growing period, starting in late summer, heavy watering (and feeding) is necessary. When the shoots are fully formed, apply a potash-rich fertiliser. The period of growth is rather short, but the shoots grow extremely quickly.

▲ There are a great many varieties of the warm-growing *Dendrobium-hybrids*, and they are not hard to grow, as long as the correct methods are followed.

◄ *Dendrobium Stardust* is a *Dendrobium nobile*-hybrid with true cool-growing ancestry, but is remarkably adaptable.

Cultivation

► *Dendrobium
nobile-hybrids* can
be grown cool, and
in flower colour
they range from
warm colours to
brilliant white.

Temperature, light and humidity

Roughly speaking *Dendrobium* can be divided
into two main groups as far as cultivation is
concerned (conditions which differ from these
should be followed up in reference books or
researched via the Internet). The first group
requires cool temperatures with plenty of light,
which is usually rather difficult to achieve in
many homes. The second group flourishes in
warm conditions; such species also like light,
but with high humidity. From early spring to the
end of summer, neither group is able to
tolerate any direct mid-day sun, so they should
definitely be kept in the shade. (If the leaves
take on any red colour this is a sign of too
much light, although this can also be the result
of root damage.) In the autumn and winter they
should be exposed to as much light as possible,
since this encourages the onset of flowering.
'Cool-growing' orchids prefer a temperature of
20–25°C (68–77°F) during the day from spring
until autumn and around 14°C (57°F) in the
winter, which is mostly their dormant period.
At night the temperature should preferably be

lowered to around 5°C (41°F) and can even be
allowed to fall to zero. Many of the cool-
growing Dendrobiums shed their leaves at the
end of the growing period.

Overwintering at low temperatures requires
economical watering (at most spray once and do
not water!). Overwintering at too high a
temperature can often mean that no flowers will
form during the next growing period. The warm-
growing orchids are comfortable at 25°C (77°F),
a temperature they can support all year round
and which should only be slightly lower at night.
High humidity is necessary for both, although
those preferring higher temperatures are more
dependent on it.

Watering

During the growing period, it is important to
water generously, although the compost must
be dried out repeatedly from time to time, to
avoid root-rot. The growing period begins with
increased root formation. Additionally, spray on
warm, sunny days in the morning. During the
winter and/or during dormancy keep watering
to a level which ensures that the compost does
not completely dry out.

► *Dendrobium*
De Hinchey retains
the typical shape
and colour of
*Dendrobium
phalaenopsis*. The
latter should not
be confused with
the moth orchids
(*Phalaenopsis*).

Antelope dendrobiums

**Some dendrobiums have petals which
turn upwards and which resemble
antelope horns. Well-known examples are
Dendrobium antennatum, *D. canaliculatum*,
D. stratiotes and *D. lineale*, which come
from Papua New Guinea. While these
can be grown indoors, hybrids of these
species are easier. All require a tropical
warm climate. They feel very comfortable
between 18–25°C (64–77°F) and do not
really need a dormant period.**

In the case of the cool-growing dendrobiums,
mostly hybrids of the *Dendrobium nobile* group,
almost no watering and only occasional
spraying is necessary during the dormant
period. These plants almost need a 'shock' in
order to flower: a sharp fall in temperature
and/or a pronounced lack of moisture over
several weeks. Above all, the modern Yamamoto
hybrids which mostly come from Japan – they
can be recognised from their relatively thick
pseudobulbs, while the pseudobulbs of
Dendrobium nobile and their direct descendants
are rather slender – are happy with a period of
dryness without needing more than a slight fall
in temperature. For species which grow at a
warm temperature (*Dendrobium phalaenopsis*
and hybrids), a temporary reduction in the
temperature of about 5°C (9°F) is sufficient
(in cases where there is a persistent lack of
flowering lower the temperature and hold back
on watering). The period of dormancy should
certainly be introduced only after the

formation and maturing of the pseudobulbs.
If budding occurs, raise the temperature and
increase watering.

Ventilation

Fresh air and air movement are important.
However, while orchids which grow at cool
temperatures are indifferent to ventilation at
every stage of their development, in the case
of warm-growing dendrobiums cold air or
even a draught can lead to a loss of buds.

Feeding

Nearly all dendrobiums (the botanical species
being the exception) need watering at least
once a week with an orchid fertiliser during the
growing period, after which they should be fed
at every third watering. In the meantime, half
the previous amount of fertiliser can be
sprayed on the leaves and aerial roots, or even
better underneath them, with an atomiser.

Repotting and compost

When the pot becomes too small and new
shoots and roots grow out of the container,
repotting is necessary. All dendrobiums prefer
small pots and are usually also mainly sold in
them, so unhealthy roots are only rarely
encountered. When repotting it is therefore
mostly necessary to cut back healthy roots, for
which there would no longer be room in the
new pot. In the new container there should be
room for two new roots. As *Dendrobium* has
rather short rhizomes, the new pot should not
be much bigger than the old one.

Because the pot can become unstable due to
the long pseudobulbs, use pebbles for drainage.
Expanded clay pellets are also suitable, but
remember to ensure that a small additional
amount of water is always available. For
stability, tie stems together with soft raffia or
twine. Alternatively, use hanging pots or small
baskets, and allow the stems to hang down.
The compost must be firm in structure
(Type A, see page 24).

▼ The so-called
***Dendrobium* Emma-
varieties** have
greenish-yellow
flowers with a highly
contrasting lip. They
are warm-growing
orchids.

Expert tips

1 Buying

Apart from a good general condition, when buying above all look for plants which are not budding too much, especially with *D. phalaenopsis*-hybrids **1a** Specimens which are sold wrapped in plastic can later easily be damaged by *botrytis* ㉕ Where bargains are concerned disappointment is guaranteed. Because of the long flowering period, mistakes in cultivation are common, but these can be recognised from leaves with a light reddish colour, indicating root damage. With the cool-growing types there are few problems of adaptation. But it is also better to buy them when the flowering stage is well advanced.

2 Extending the flowering period

In the case of warm-growing dendrobiums, it is possible to prolong the flowering period artificially, by keeping the plants at a cooler temperature (but never lower than about 16°C/61°F), but only when the first flush of flowers has finished.

3 Bud drop

Sometimes dendrobiums lose their buds, particularly in the case of hybrids of the *D. phalaenopsis* group. The reasons for this are assumed to be similar to those with the moth orchids, but in this case there is no chance of the old shoot producing any new flowers. The buds of cool-growing dendrobiums are rather insensitive and any loss in their case will primarily be because of too much water. Dendrobiums which flower in clusters can sometimes produce additional flowers on old shoots, after they have previously refused to flower for whatever reason.

4 *Dendrobium* keikis

Many dendrobiums develop keikis (plantlets) instead of flowers, particularly when they are grown without a dormant period, but also as a consequence of serious mistakes in watering and/or root damage and low temperature. As with moth orchids, you initially need only patience. The plant should be potted only when roots and leaves have developed. *Dendrobium* keikis should be put into very small pots and using a fine compost mixture (type B, see page 24; the finer grades of proprietary orchid compost can also be used). It is better to use a very small pot without drainage than to use a larger one with drainage material.

5 My *Dendrobium* simply will not flower!

For dendrobiums that grow at cool temperatures, too much heat – when dormant – is the most frequent cause of failure to flower. With the warm-growing types, the absence of a lowering in temperature or an insufficient reduction in temperature can be responsible as well; more often,

however, the shoots simply do not develop sufficiently: of necessity, an ever smaller shoot replaces its predecessor. But only vigorous annual shoots develop flowers. So pay attention to the correct conditions for cultivation. When cultivating indoors with a rather low level of humidity there is in addition a physiological problem, caused by too little light combined with night-time temperatures which are too high. Nocturnal respiration then uses too much energy, which can no longer be replenished during the day because of a reduced ability to assimilate.

6 Can dendrobiums be kept with other houseplants?

Dendrobium can certainly be grown with other indoor plants. For varieties which grow at a cool temperature cactuses and succulents are appropriate, while for those growing at warm temperatures perhaps begonias and *Ficus repens*, the creeping rubber plant, are worth considering.

7 Is it possible to put dendrobiums outside in summer?

Possibly, but only in the case of the cool and acclimatised species and hybrids. First choose a spot half in the shade, so that the orchids can then later accustom themselves to the light and be grown in full sunlight. Always protect them from continuous rain. All warm-growing varieties should stay indoors or in the greenhouse.

8 What to watch out for in the greenhouse

Brown spots on the flowers can indicate *botrytis* infection (grey mould). The cause for this is too high humidity and too little air movement. *Botrytis* mainly occurs in the greenhouse in winter, when there may be insufficient ventilation.

The cool-growing dendrobiums are best suited for the greenhouse, as they can be provided with optimal conditions there.

This also goes for the many dwarf varieties derived from this genus. An example is *Dendrobium kingianum* 8, which is now sold more widely and which has larger and smaller variants. It flowers mainly during spring. It produces loose clusters of small flowers which are only about 1.5–2.5 cm (½–1 in) long and range from creamy white to purple-pink in colour. In addition, many display dark veins. Plants just a few years old may produce ten new shoots and flowering stems. *D. kingianum* is regarded as quite undemanding from the point of view of cultivation, but is a typical coldhouse orchid and should not be kept at too warm a temperature while in flower. It is best kept at temperatures between 4 and 14°C (39 and 57°F). Overwintering too warm or moist can inhibit flowering.

8

9 Growing epiphytically

This is not only possible, but is even highly recommended in the case of species and their cultivars which flower in clusters. Even the small varieties can be grown this way. A small amount of compost is needed for all of them. When cultivating indoors the *Dendrobium phalaenopsis* types are not suitable for tying up. In this case, it is difficult to maintain the appropriate humidity. Small baskets or hanging pots, which allow for a natural development, are better for indoors. This is, however more time-consuming, because of the need for more frequent spraying.

10 Pests and diseases*

Mistakes which result from incorrect plant care can be recognised from the state of the compost ①–⑤. Unfortunately, bud drop is not uncommon in the case of the warm-growing dendrobiums ㉔. *Botrytis* attack is possible if the plant is transported in a plastic bag ㉕. Scale insects and mealybugs are rare ㉘, ㉙, but spider mites are common ⑮, ㉝.

If there is insufficient warmth for *D. phalaenopsis*, the shoots will only grow poorly in the winter. If *D. nobile* is kept at too warm a temperature, it will grow too

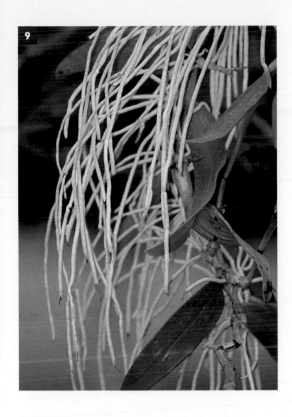

NOTE **Transferring orchids to hydroculture**

Orchids should only be repotted if they have produced a new shoot. *Phalaenopsis* have proved themselves particularly suited to experimentation. This is how to proceed: remove the compost completely and wash thoroughly. Remove damaged and dead roots, avoiding cutting into healthy roots. Always use a sharp knife or secateurs and have charcoal powder handy. Allow the plant to dry and fill the cultivation pot with washed, dried, expanded clay pellets (grade $^{8}/_{16}$). The cultivation pot should be at least 12 cm (5 in) tall. Do not plant too deeply, nor allow old roots to touch the water. Pour a little water (maximum 0.5 cm/¼ in) into the outer pot and insert the cultivation pot. Do not simply top up with water from above. A sheet of plastic film that reduces water loss through transpiration will encourage the plant to put on growth.

quickly. In both cases fungal and bacterial infections can easily result ⑥–⑧.

▌▌ Hydroculture

Hydroculture is better suited to the greenhouse varieties than to the cool-growing ones. When using expanded clay pellets make sure the water can drain well. Adaptation will then occur largely without problems. As the plants must be repeatedly allowed to dry out (small pots), indicators for water level and humidity are no great help. The plants must be truly dry before each watering (pay particular attention to the roots). If rot occurs, it is better to repot in fresh compost using small containers. Do not use container pots, which are the custom commercially, either with expanded clay pellets or when growing in compost. Repot as early as possible, but only when there is a new shoot.

*The numbers refer to the Appendix, page 135ff.

Vanda

Vanda, Ascocentrum, etc.

Once seen this orchid is not easily forgotten; *Vanda* is a particularly exclusive plant. And because these marvellous orchids only grow very slowly, they will also probably remain very exclusive. Blue (violet) vandas are the most widely cultivated. They are mostly a radiant, powerful blue, which nevertheless appears filigreed, or even almost transparent. There are also vandas in white, yellow, pink and purple. The flowers last for an unusually long time, even when cut. *Vanda* is the national flower of Singapore. It is native to tropical Thailand, subtropical Nepal, Burma, south China, and Borneo and neighbouring islands. It also grows above 2500 m (8000 ft) in the Himalayas.

Vanda orchids are not entirely straightforward when it comes to cultivation and require much attention. However, if they are well cared for they will produce flowering shoots twice a year. The flowers are long-lived and last for six weeks or more. Plants of the hybrid genus *Ascocenda* (= *Ascocentrum* × *Vanda*) are somewhat easier to grow, because most varieties grow and flower particularly readily.

▲ *Vanda* **Madam Rafflaus** × **Pinpinol** × **Gordon Dillon**, a hybrid with complex parentage. Like all vandas, it is best grown in a small wooden basket.

◀ Vandas need little compost when grown in a small wooden basket, and can be mixed with other epiphytes to decorative effect – as here with tillandsias.

► Another *Ascocenda* hybrid (***Ascocenda Udomchai*** × ***Vanda Bangkapi Gold***). This plant is sold in all colours – white, blue, pink or lilac, even different shades of yellow.

◄ The natural shape of the parent species *Ascocentrum miniatum* can be seen in this ***Ascocenda***. Unlike the species it has somewhat smaller flowers but in great numbers, and branching flower stems are also possible. It is not difficult to grow.

◄ A *Vanda* hybrid, this time a **cross with *Vanda Kultana Gold***. The Kultana Orchids Company of Thailand is one of the largest exporters of vandas and other hybrids to Europe and the USA. Cultivation hints (in English) are also available at www.orchid.in.th.

113

Cultivation

Temperature, light and humidity

The various climatic zones from which this group comes also imply different conditions for cultivation. For cool greenhouses and conservatories the most suitable are hybrids of *Vanda coerulea* (blue) and *Vanda/Ascocentrum* hybrids (*Ascocenda*). These also flourish in a cool, light room and in the winter it is then necessary to spray only rarely. The roots begin to grow again once the days start becoming longer – then spraying and fertilising can be increased and the temperatures can rise. In winter this group needs at least 13–15°C (32–59°F) and in summer up to 30°C (86°F). The warm-growing varieties need high humidity. Glass vases and aquaria make good mini-greenhouses.

Generally, indoor cultivation is not easy. Success is more likely if the plant can be hung in a container. At least then the problem of humidity is easy to solved, as the bottom of the container can be filled with a layer of damp expanded clay pellets.

All varieties like as much light as possible, but not direct sunlight (if the light is too bright, screen the window with gauze). Warm-growing varieties – including the large-flowered commercially produced hybrids in particular – can stay indoors all year at a minimum temperature of 20°C (68°F). The temperature should not be allowed to fall much below that at night.

◀ A large glass vase offers the ideal environment for the sensitive roots of *Vanda* and related hybrids. The water reserves in the soil provide the necessary humidity.

NOTE The growth and cultivation of vandas in European nurseries has also been successful. Such plants are mostly more 'robust' than those imported directly. Incidentally, vandas also form plantlets, mostly at the base of the plant. A plantlet can be removed if its roots are about 8 to 10 cm (3 to 4 in) long. This should be done with even more care than with other orchids, so that the parent plant is not damaged. As ever, sharp, sterile tools should be used (sterilise beforehand by passing through a flame), and the resulting incision treated with charcoal powder.

Watering (without compost)
Vandas are often sold in a wooden basket with little compost, sometimes with just a few small pieces of charcoal or coconut. How can these be watered sufficiently? Above all, frequent spraying is important. In addition, the plants should be completely submerged in water at least once a week (along with the container/basket and roots). The water must be tepid and you should proceed very carefully so as not to break the roots. At the same time, make sure that no water remains in the leaf axils, otherwise the plants will rot.

If complete submersion is either not possible or desirable there is a simple alternative. Some roots – always in rotation – can be placed into small water tubes, like those used for transporting cut orchids. After about three weeks, switch these to different roots. The roots must be allowed to dry off and resume their function as aerial roots, otherwise they will rot. Although *Vanda* has no pseudobulbs and therefore also no definite period of dormancy, watering should be substantially reduced in winter. These orchids (at least the warm-growing hybrids that are commercially available) actually grow all year round; the temperature should nevertheless be reduced at night by at least 5°C (9°F) to induce flower formation.

Ventilation
Air movement without draughts is a prerequisite for successful cultivation. Cold air from loose windows or in the greenhouse causes growth disorders.

Feeding
Feeding should basically be moderate, at best in a weak concentration with every watering (even orchid fertilisers should be reduced by half of the amount recommended by the manufacturer). Commercial 'organic' liquid fertilisers are well suited to *Vanda*. Home-made fertilisers may also be suitable. While the flowers are developing, feeding can be somewhat increased.

Repotting and compost
Repotting is rarely necessary. Plant in a new (wooden) basket only when absolutely necessary. The thick, mostly very long aerial roots can scarcely fit into normal pots. The old basket can simply be placed inside the new container. Use only coarse compost material: pieces of bark, cork, charcoal or coconut chippings. Equally suitable is a mixture of pine bark, peat and polystyrene beads with added pieces of charcoal. Long aerial roots should on no account be cut off, but should be carefully reinserted in the container or run alongside it.

▼ *Vanda* roots can occasionally be fed by using small tubes for cut flowers. However, only about 10 per cent of the healthy roots should be treated like this.

Expert tips

1 Buying

Do not allow yourself to be tempted by the beautiful flowers. Only buy an orchid if you are really well prepared for the additional expenditure necessary for its cultivation. In choosing it is important to pay attention to healthy roots. And the plant should not be budding too much. Also look for pests, as scale insects are very widespread.

2 My *Vanda* simply will not flower!

If vandas or *Ascocentrum* do not flower, it is as a rule the poor general condition of the plants that is responsible. The only thing that will help here is a change in the conditions in which the plants are cultivated. In the case of vigorous but non-flowering plants, lowering the temperature by about 5°C (9°F) can be successful.

3 Can vandas be grown with other houseplants?

Vandas are somewhat 'solitary' and also require their own environment (e.g. a glass container). Proximity to other houseplants does not provide enough humidity.

4 Can vandas be put outside in the summer?

A 'summer holiday' only makes sense for those species which come from cooler regions. They must be allowed to grow accustomed to the light slowly, but will eventually even be able to tolerate strong sunlight. They must be protected from continuous rain and cold and wet weather, and must also be brought indoors again in good time in late summer.

5 What to watch out for in the greenhouse

If the greenhouse has the right temperature, cultivation will naturally be much easier there. Light and humidity rarely cause problems. If it is not possible to ventilate, 'artificial' air movement is important.

2

Shade is mostly only necessary from late spring, and should be discontinued again at the right moment, as light is the most important factor in the cultivation of this group. *Vanda coerulea* and its hybrids need a cool, dry dormant period in the winter. This begins when the root tips and the shoots stop growing. These plants also do not need as much light as other vandas from the hot and humid tropics.

6 Growing epiphytically

Naturally, vandas can be mounted on a piece of wood or cork bark. For long stems use a long, rather narrow piece and tie the plant to it several times using something soft (e.g. nylon stockings). No compost, or very little, is necessary; moss is more suitable.

7 Terminal cuttings

Vandas often develop roots in the upper third of the plant. Root formation can also be encouraged by using moss, which must always be kept moist. Finally, if enough roots are present, the cutting may be separated from the parent plant and allowed to continue growing on its own (attach to bark or plant in a basket).

8 Pests and diseases*

The most frequent (and also avoidable) mistake is providing insufficient humidity. The result is root damage, and ultimately the whole plant will dry out. It is also necessary to watch out for scale insects and mealybugs ㉘, ㉙ as well as spider mites ⑮, ㉝. Unfortunately, it is not unusual to experience loss of the (pea-sized) buds, and there are often several reasons for this ㉔. If transported in a plastic bag, sometimes the flowers will suffer an attack of *botrytis* ㉕, in which case the damage will only be visible once you get home.

9 Hydroculture

Vandas are not really suited to hydroculture. When grown in this way, their roots grow down into the layer of expanded clay pellets in the container (glass vase, aquarium) and also continue to grow there.

---

*The numbers refer to the Appendix, page 135ff.

6

Zygopetalum

Expert tips

1 Buying

Spots on the leaves are almost always normal with this genus and should not deter the prospective purchaser, but they should on no account be wet and rotting. Only buy this orchid if you are able to offer it the appropriate conditions.

2 My *Zygopetalum* simply will not flower!

There is really only one explanation. Most well-developed plants are kept at too warm a temperature. A successful remedy is to lower the temperature to induce a period of dormancy.

3   Can *Zygopetalum* be put outside in summer?

A period outside in semi-shade, in a protected place, is to be recommended for indoor plants in summer. Otherwise they should stay in the greenhouse.

4   What to watch out for in the greenhouse

No particular measures are necessary in the greenhouse, although the soft leaves and flowers should be protected from slugs and snails. These orchids have adapted to a cool-temperate climate.

5   Growing epiphytically

The thick roots – at least when cultivated indoors – are happier in a pot, although *Zygopetalum* is actually epiphytic. When mounting on bark, use plenty of compost and moss.

6   What happens if they are not fed enough?

If *Zygopetalum* plants do not receive their optimal supply of nutrients they will only develop small annual shoots. The cause could be no new roots, a need for repotting or extra feeding, or being kept too dry. These 'emergency shoots' do not flower, and usually die.

7   Pests and diseases*

Zygopetalum species and hybrids have a tendency to suffer from fungal infections ⑦, ⑧, mostly recognisable as blackish brown sunken spots on the leaves **7**. Fresh air and air movement can prevent this. If as a precaution you are not spraying the leaves directly from mid-day onwards, do not spray at all on cool, humid days. Spider mites ⑮, ㉝ proliferate especially at low humidity; if the air is too dry there is also the danger of attack by mealybugs and scale insects ㉙, ㉘. Sometimes the plant is infected with viruses ㊱, in which case an expert should be consulted.

8   Hydroculture

Zygopetalum is suitable for hydroculture. However, the fleshy roots must be thoroughly washed out before transfer to hydroculture, and with expanded clay pellets not too much compost should be used. The dormant period must be strictly observed; the humidity remaining in the compost will still be sufficient for several weeks.

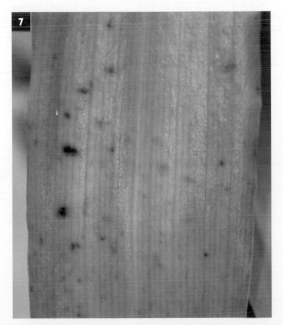

---

*The numbers refer to the Appendix, page 135ff.

Epidendrum

The genus name *Epidendrum* is derived from Greek and means 'growing on trees'. *Encyclia* is related to *Epidendrum*. This name is also derived from Greek and means 'clasp/embrace', referring to the way the lip and column of the flower are fused together. Both genera reach an impressive height. However, in most outlets only a few plants are available (specialist orchid growers offer considerably more choice). Most are cultivars of *Epidendrum radicans*, also known as *E. ibaguense*. One cultivar name has established itself as a term for this group: *Ballerina orchids*. While the species itself has very long pseudobulbs (more than 1 m/3 ft in length), the cultivars are quite compact, but even these may still reach 60 cm (24 in) tall. *Epidendrum* Ballerina Purple (violet), Snow (white), Tropical (yellow, lined with orange), Fireball (red/orange), Tiffany (reddish) and Yellow are popular forms.

These hybrids develop pseudobulbs with leathery shiny leaves in two rows and produce their flowers – for many weeks on end – in compact inflorescences with a stem up to 40 cm (16 in) tall.

Of the genus *Encyclia*, only *E. cochleata* is widely available, an indigenous form from South America with an unusually long flowering period, even as a pot plant. Incidentally, this species used to be included within *Epidendrum*, and in old orchid books you will therefore find them under this name.

► *Epidendrum* **Ballerina Yellow** (left) and *Epidendrum radicans* (right) show the variety within this widespread species.

Cultivation

Temperature, light and humidity

Epidendrum and *Encyclia* are best suited to normal room temperature, and in summer do best at 18–25°C (64–77°F) by day, at night around 15°C (59°F), somewhat lower in winter. All in all, both genera are very adaptable and require average light. They are also not very fussy about humidity.

Watering

As long as the growing period and the very short dormancy are taken into account, watering is no real problem. These orchids need less water than you might think. They should not, however, be allowed to dry out either.

Ventilation

Since *Epidendrum* and *Encyclia* are really easy to care for, lots of fresh air (even when the temperature is only a few degrees above zero) is an advantage, and can prevent fungal disease.

Feeding

When using orchid fertiliser it should be given at every third watering. Around the end of the growing period use a flower fertilizer as well, but reduce the recommended dosage by at least half.

Repotting and compost

Do not use pots that are too big. It is better to repot these orchids frequently. They can be propagated by division: just cut the plant into two or more parts (do not try to pull them apart, as the

Fragrant orchids

This *Epidendrum* Green Hornet (= *E. lancifolium* × *E. cochleatum*), but also many other forms of *Epidendrum* are often referred to as 'fragrant' orchids. In fact there are fragrant species in almost all genera. Commonly available are: *Oncidium ornithorhynchum* and its hybrids, × *Miltonidium* 'Hawaiian Sunset', many forms of *Miltonia*, *Phalaenopsis* 'Liodoro' and many others including all *Zygopetalum*.

pseudobulbs easily break off). Any orchid compost is suitable (to mix it yourself use type A, see page 24). With *Encyclia cochleata* two newly sprouting pseudobulbs should fit into a single pot.

◄ *Epidendrum radicans* **hybrids** are not especially striking in the proportion of plant to flower. They tend to develop plantlets. A plant like the one shown here urgently needs repotting.

Expert tips

1 Buying

These orchids are frequently offered in garden centres and DIY stores or as special offers. These are fine unless you are looking for a specific variety or colour. The plants are robust enough to remain healthy even in such outlets.

2 Flower and keiki formation

The flowers are small, each only about 2 cm (¾ in) acrosss, and develop in clusters at the tips of shoots, from early spring until

early autumn. Sufficient light is required for them to flower, and it is a mistake to position them somewhere too dark and too warm. Keiki formation often follows if you cut the tips off the shoots after flowering, when they are fully dry.

They should not be too small, however, and need to have developed many roots of their own. The best time for this is spring. Keiki formation is rare in *Encyclia cochleata* and results mainly from mistakes in care (too much water, no dormancy), but otherwise the cultivation of both genera is similar. However, with *Encyclia* dormancy is important.

3 Is is possible to put these plants outside in summer?

These orchids can be placed outdoors from late spring until the end of summer, in a semi-shaded position in the garden or on the balcony.

4 Pests and diseases*

Mainly scale insects and mealybugs ㉘, ㉙, more rarely spider mites ⑮, ㉝. Fungal diseases and bacteria ⑥–⑧ usually only appear as a consequence of incorrect care.

5 Hydroculture

Both plants are suitable for cultivation in hydro clay and expanded clay pellets from the start of the growing season. Both then require a substantial period of dormancy.

---

*The numbers refer to the Appendix page 135ff.

Calanthe

This beautiful, mostly terrestrial genus is mainly from Asia, with just a few of the almost 150 species occurring in South America. Most of those available are deciduous, although there are also evergreen species. The highly appropriate name is derived from the Greek 'kalos' meaning 'beautiful' and 'anthe' meaning 'flower'.

► *Calanthe vestita* used to be popular as a very long-lasting cut flower. Today it is usually offered as a pot plant.

▼ *Calanthe* **Hexem Gem** should be grown like the other calanthes, although it does grow quite as big.

◄ *Calanthe* **Sedenii 'Harrisii'** is derived from *C. Veitchii* (= *C. rosea* × *vestita*), which was the first orchid cross ever made in England. It has been available since 1878.

Cultivation

▶ *Calanthe triplictra* can grow to one metre (3 ft) tall. It is multi-flowered, evergreen, and has a wide distribution.

Temperature, light and humidity

Calanthe need plenty of warmth (around 20°C/68°F), semi-shade and high humidity. After the leaves have fallen off they should be kept cooler and completely dry.

Watering

During the growing period, plenty of water is required, but avoid saturation. Towards the end of the growing period – when the pseudobulbs are swollen and firm – and when flowering, reduce the amount of water considerably, but do not allow the pseudobulbs to shrivel. After flowering, stop watering completely. You can even remove the plant from the pot and store it dry, wrapped in paper. However, you need to watch for a new shoot, which indicates fresh growth. Then pot it up again and/or slowly increase the amount of water. New shoots rot easily.

Feeding

Calanthes are sturdy orchids, which develop a pseudobulb, leaves and flowers relatively quickly. Therefore feed at the start of the growing season using an orchid fertiliser at every second watering, according to instructions, from summer onwards at every third watering, and eventually reduce the dosage by half. Too little fertiliser results in small new shoots and no flowers. As soon as the leaves turn yellow, stop feeding. If you keep calanthes drier, the shoot matures and the following season's flowers are built. The leaves are shed completely. The actual full dormancy only starts at the end of the flowering time, from late autumn into winter.

Repotting and compost

Calanthes should really be repotted every year, in rich compost but in small pots.

Always wait until the new growth appears and be careful as the small shoots break easily. No additional drainage is required. Use any orchid compost mixed ⅓ with conventional potting compost (DIY compost type C, see page 24).

▶ The flowering stalk of this *Calanthe* is emerging from the leafless pseudobulbs. Last season's dry leaf base is still visible on the right-hand pseudobulb.

Expert tips

1 Buying

You can often buy a calanthe that has finished flowering fairly cheap, as only a few sellers are aware of the true value of a dormant plant. Watch out for signs of fungal disease, and do not buy plants with wet, rotten parts on the pseudobulb. Dry leaves, on the other hand, are normal.

2 Flower and keiki formation

Calanthes sometimes develop keikis at the top of the pseudobulb. When they are big enough, they are easily removed

and treated just like the parent plant. On the flower stem, scale-like, dry covering leaves develop beneath the flower. These do not cause any harm, but look scruffy and can be safely removed.

3 Can *Calanthe* be kept with other houseplants?

Sometimes calanthes are offered in a pot together with a fern. This is done to conceal the naked pseudobulb, but in general it only causes problems. As both plants have different watering and growth requirements, it is better to remove the fern.

4 Outside in summer?

Because of the soft, sensitive leaves it is best not to grow them outside.

5 Pests and diseases*

The main enemy are spider mites ⑮, ㉝, as well as fungal diseases and bacteria ⑥–⑧. Leaf drop at the end of the growing period is normal ⑨.

6 Hydroculture

The strict dormancy makes cultivation in hydro-clay or expanded clay pellets difficult, and watering does not really cause any major problems. In general, it is possible though with this terrestrial genus. Expanded clay pellets may also be used as compost supplement in normal cultivation.

---

*The numbers refer to the Appendix page 135ff.

Phaius

Phaius tankervilliae is one of the most impressive exotic orchids, but for a long time was rarely available. Besides its imposing size – it can reach the impressive height of 150 cm (54 in) when in flower – that deterred some growers, plants in cultivation often developed visible black-brown leaf spots. This was possibly caused by a virus in the original species. Since then, virus-free plants have been bred, and it is available once again. There are many new cultivars.

In nature the genus *Phaius* is found in mountain forests from tropical China, through Asia to Northern Australia, Africa and Madagascar. It is evergreen with large, soft leaves.

◄ ▲ The colour range of the new **Phaius** hybrids is astonishing. The plants are not as huge anymore, and will therefore soon be some of the most popular orchids.

Cultivation

Temperature, light and humidity

In summer *Phaius* prefers to be grown in
shade, without direct sunlight, and kept warm.
In winter they need as much light as possible.
As the temperature should never sink below
15°C (59°F) the plants are ideal for a
conservatory (temperature in summer
20–28°C/68–82°F by day, a little lower at
night; in winter 18–20°C/64–68°F during
the day and around 15°C/59°F at night).
At the end of the growing period, a
three-week dry period is sufficient to
induce flowering.

Watering

During the growing period, mostly from spring
onwards, keep the plants fairly moist. The
leaves should be kept dry, as water can easily
lead to leaf spots. At all cost avoid moisture
build-up, and
in winter
water only in
moderation.

$NOTE$ **Spathoglottis
Caractea®**

These cultivation hints are also relevant
for *Spathoglottis* Caractea®, which is
now often available. It can flower in
all seasons and remains attractive
by virtue of its evergreen leaves.
The plant likes warmth, in winter
around 18–20°C (64–68°F), in summer
20–28°C (68–82°F). Dormancy is
not very pronounced; in winter just
keep the plant a little cooler. Choose
a light position, but without direct
sunlight, and do not let the plant
dry out completely. It can be fed
generously, and feeding also extends
flowering.

Feeding

During the growing season feed at
every second watering with orchid
fertiliser at the advised rate. In
autumn and winter, feed at every
third watering.

Repotting and compost

The right moment to repot is when
new growth appears, or immediately
after flowering. Division may also
stimulate the plant to produce flowers.
Plant in tall containers, ideally, in any kind
of orchid compost (to mix type B yourself,
see page 24). Good drainage is important
to avoid the waterlogging that can quickly
cause root damage. *Phaius* can also be
planted in beds in the garden in
some regions.

◄ *Phaius
tankervilliae*, at
over one metre
(3 ft) tall, is
a truly impressive
plant that is at home
in the conservatory
as well as in
botanical
collections.

Expert tips

1 Buying

This plant grows large quite fast, so think about the space available before buying. Transport with care, as *Phaius* orchids are easily damaged, especially the flowers. Look out for spots on the leaves **1**.

2 Outside in summer?

Not recommended, as the night temperature is often too low.

3 Pests and diseases*

Besides fungus and bacterial diseases ⑥–⑧, scale insects and mealybugs can occur ㉘, ㉙, as can, at low humidity, red spider mites ⑮, ㉝. Thrips are a rarer problem. Large plants with many leaves sometimes develop spots on leaves produced the previous year. These can be removed or the affected areas cut off (only use a disinfected, clean knife or scissors).

4 Hydroculture

Both cultivated species are suitable, as *Phaius* is a terrestrial plant. On the other hand, the roots are very sensitive to wet. Hybrids of *Phaius humblotii* **4** cope well with warmth and therefore make good houseplants.

For *Phaius* ensure that the water level is adjusted as low as possible and allow a sufficiently long dry period.

---

* The numbers refer to the Appendix, page 135ff.

Common Problems*

Problems with the compost

① White or grey deposits on the surface

Water – particularly hard water – leaves salt deposits behind as it evaporates. If this affects the aerial roots it can harm them, especially if these are very thin.

② Fungal growth on the surface

This happens mainly with bark or peat, often after repotting, is not usually troublesome, and normally disappears quite rapidly.

③ Algae, moss, liverworts on the surface

Caused by high (too high?) humidity. Dry out and renew the surface layer.

④ Springtails – small colourless invertebrates, about 1–4 mm (¹⁄₂₅–⁴⁄₂₅ in) long

Springtails (Collembola) may appear especially in soil-rich compost (they jump when watered). These primitive creatures live in damp sites and feed on rotting plant material. They are wingless, 1–4 mm (¹⁄₂₅–⁴⁄₂₅ in) long with a whitish, sometimes silvery black colour, and a characteristic spring organ underneath. Not really a problem, but in large numbers they can damage root tips and young plant tissues. Treatment: keep compost dry.

⑤ Fungus gnats

These tiny black flies, about 3 mm (³⁄₂₅ in) long, are sometimes disturbed when watering or moving orchids. They breed in damp, peat-rich compost or sphagnum, which contains their pale grey larvae, about 7 mm (⁷⁄₂₅ in) long. These larvae eat the roots and base of the stems. If possible, the plants should be kept drier. The larvae are often found with fungal infections on the thick roots of *Phalaenopsis*. They lay their eggs on weak plants or those affected by fungi. Fungus gnats dislike yellow and can be discouraged by the use of yellow paper or stickers or a yellow dish full of water to which a few drops of washing up liquid have been added. They either stick tight, or drown. Another method is to use a couple of butterwort plants (*Pinguicula*) to trap them.

Leaves, roots and pseudobulbs

⑥ Brown or rotting roots

Velamen mouldy or soft and gooey. Usually caused by too much water, often combined with a low compost temperature. The answer is normally to water less often. Bacterial and fungal infections can follow, and some orchids also show damage to the leaves, such as crumpling, caused by irregular water supply to the tissues.

▲ ② Fungal growth on bark is easy to see, and is quite normal, as long as it doesn't get out of hand.

▼ ③ Mosses are not usually encouraged, but they can sometimes be helpful, for example by protecting the roots from salt accumulation.

*Numbers in circles refer to information given under 'Pests and Diseases' in the relevant chapters.

▲ ⑥ Using transparent pots makes it easier to check the water content.

⑦ **Leaves and shoots rot from the base or centre, or show dark indentations in the surface. Pseudobulbs turn brown or black.**
A sign that the roots are too moist and/or soil temperature is too low. In most cases such plants cannot be saved.
Often results in an attack on leaves, stems and flowers by different fungi, including *Botrytis cinerea* that grows on all plant parts. In high humidity the characteristic signs are mouse grey felty fungus spores on the affected parts, also showing as dark spots on the flowers. Black fungus may also appear on the roots, rhizomes, stems and leaves. The fungi penetrate the orchids and exude poison, softening the plant tissues and killing the plant relatively quickly. If an infection of this sort is suspected, consult an expert.

⑧ **Leaves become translucent**
Can be caused by different bacteria – hard to identify. Bacteria are unicellular organisms that can move in water, and multiply rapidly by division in a matter of minutes under warm, damp conditions. They cannot damage healthy plants, but can infect open wounds or splits. *Erwinia carotovora* and *E. cypripedii* cause damp rot, which appears as soft dull yellow spots on the leaves. The rot normally starts on the leaf bases, then spreads over the whole leaf, eventually leaving just a soft mass. It can spread quickly over the whole plant. Other bacteria often attack at the same time. With sympodial orchids you can try to remove the infected pseudobulbs, ideally disinfecting the knife (e.g. in a flame) before each cut.

▼ ⑦ Typical heart rot in *Phalaenopsis*, usually the result of too much water, but sometimes caused by too low temperatures.

⑨ **Leaves dry out and fall off**
For those, such as *Calanthe* and *Lycaste*, with a definite dormant period this is normal, as low temperature or drought is a feature of this period. All plants lose individual old leaves, as they produce new ones. Lack of water is rarely the cause – more often too much water.

⑩ **Leaves turn pale green or yellow-green**
Lack of light and nitrogen produce yellowing and leaf fall. The plants may also be suffering from sucking pests, especially spider mites. A sign is if the leaves droop even though the compost is moist.

⑪ **Sticky leaves**
Stickiness is usually caused by exudations from aphids, scale insects or whiteflies, though sticky patches on stems can result from cool temperatures.

⑫ **Water drops on the leaf tips or edges**
This is a normal phenomenon (guttation) in some species, for example *Phalaenopsis*. This can increase if the soil is damp and the humidity is high.

⑬ **Leaves crumpled or rolled, preceded or accompanied by indented lines, mostly parallel to the veins**
Usually caused by root damage (see earlier), and can result in a characteristic pattern in *Miltonia* and intergeneric hybrids (see photo). The humidity may be too low. Crumpled or deformed leaves usually result from pest attack (often spider mites) or viral infection.

⑭ **Symptoms only on young leaves**

Pale or whitish green between the veins on young leaves (veins remaining green) is a sign of iron deficiency. Often happens in hydroculture, especially in summer and if the pH of the solution goes above 6. Add an iron-rich fertiliser to the solution or in water.

⑮ **Irregular pale spots on leaves**

Spider mites or aphids.

⑯ **Yellow patches of varied size**

Usually a result of cold water on warm foliage.

⑰ **Leaves go brown, starting at the tip**

The air may be too dry, or there may be a lack of nutrients (often a lack of potassium in the case of *Cymbidium*).

⑱ **Leaves turn brown at the edges**

Salt concentration too high, either because of incorrect or too frequent watering, or use of water that is too hard. Either repot, or flush out the soil with pure, soft water.

⑲ **More general browning**

Often caused by misuse of plant spray compounds, such as those used for polishing foliage. Can also be caused by burns from overheating.

⑳ **Brownish, or corky patches, not generally spreading**

Caused not by parasites, but by inappropriate siting or too frequent watering and compost that is too damp under high humidity.

㉑ **Pale spots, becoming corky and brown**

Leaves may also be misshapen. Tiny brownish black spots (droppings) on fallen leaves are usually a sign of thrips. The same symptoms may be visible on buds and flowers. If no pests, this could also be caused by viruses.

㉒ **Leaves turn red fairly evenly over the whole surface**

Too intense sunlight (whole shoot may turn red). Supply more shade. May be caused by low temperature.

㉓ **Leaves turn red mainly at the edges**

Phosphorus (on old leaves) or copper (young leaves) deficiency, common in *Phalaenopsis*. Treat using appropriate fertiliser.

Buds and flowers

㉔ **Bud and/or flower drop**

This often happens with newly acquired orchids as a reaction to the change in growing conditions (light, temperature, humidity, water regime). Water shortage can be caused by root damage. Other possible causes are the effects of smoke and ethylene, or lack of light in autumn and winter. In general, an indication of unsuitable conditions.

㉕ **Mouldy buds or flowers**

Often caused by *Botrytis*. The first sign is often dark grey spots on the flowers.

㉖ **Crumpled or deformed flowers**

Usually the result of a virus; flowers often also show coloured patches and stripes. Also brown stripes in the tissues.

▲ ⑬ Crumpled leaf caused by water supply problems resulting from root damage.

▼ ⑯, ⑰, ⑱, ⑲ This kind of damage is typical of many orchids, and has many causes. Note whether the damage spreads, and look first for an invertebrate pest. Next, consider problems of water or nutrient supply, and lastly the humidity.

▲ ㉕ *Botrytis* on a moth orchid (*Phalaenopsis*). Often caused by too high humidity and cold.

▼ ㉗ Aphids can quickly become a plague. Whether green, black or yellow, they are easily dealt with.

▼ ㉘ Scale insects on a *Cattleya* leaf. They can often also be found in the outer layer of pseudobulbs.

Pests and viruses

㉗ Aphids

Aphids are small winged or unwinged insects about 1–4 mm (¹⁄₂₅–¹⁄₂₅ in) long, with long legs and antennae. In houses and greenhouses they usually reproduce parthenogenetically – the females produce young aphids without the need for fertilisation. They tend to congregate on young shoots, soft leaves and flowers. Aphids feed directly from the vascular bundles and accumulate so-called honeydew. Aphid attack increases the danger of virus infection. They attack many other plants and fly in from outdoors in late spring and summer. They can be tackled with insecticides if necessary, preferably administered by spray, and biological control is also possible.

㉘ Scale insects

Scale insects are small to medium-sized insects in which the males and females differ greatly in size and shape (males are however rare, and parthenogenesis is the norm). The body of the female is covered by a waxy layer which gives good protection and also makes scale insects difficult to treat. Reproduction is via eggs and takes only a few weeks. Only the young larvae move, while the adults sit tight on the orchids. Hard and soft scale insects are the two groups involved. The former have an armoured body and they suck juice from the cells, rather than from the vascular vessels (the most important for orchids is the palm scale insect). Soft scale insects are usually associated with honeydew production and sooty mould.

The best way to control them is to attack the mobile larvae. It is sometimes possible to scrape the adults off the foliage before spraying with insecticide. But be careful not to damage the leaves – a soft toothbrush or soapy sponge is sometimes useful. Repeat the spraying in 1–2 weeks or according to instructions.

㉙ Mealybugs

Mealybugs are related to scale insects but have no shield, protecting themselves with a mealy whitish layer of wax. Two species are common on orchids: the citrus mealybug (oval, dark yellow to yellow-brown with waxy growths and short thick threads around the edges, honeydew producer) and the longtailed mealybug (oval, reddish to orange, with long tail threads and profuse honeydew production). The honeydew is often followed by mould. Mealybugs hide under the leaves, sit on flower stems and petals and in the outer layer of bulbs. They are relatively unaffected by chemical products, and it is best to treat them early. It is worth trying different products at intervals. Biological control is probably a better method.

㉚ Slugs and snails

These molluscs are mainly active at dusk or at night and spend the day under bark, pots or between plants. They produce slime and eat almost any green plant material. The eggs are laid in the substrate, and they can reproduce quickly. Both slugs and snails attack orchids, especially *Phalaenopsis* and other soft-leaved genera. They are

particularly partial to young soft plant tissues, including flowers. Snail and slug damage to roots and the lower parts of plants can create wounds that act as entry points for fungal attack.
They can be tackled using slug pellets and iron preparations, or trapped for example by placing cucumber slices between the plants.

㉛ Fungus gnats
See under ⑤.

㉜ Thrips
These small (about 1 mm/¹⁄₂₅ in long) slim, brownish black insects with characteristically fringed wings usually sit on the undersides of the leaves. The unwinged larvae are hard to locate. Typical signs of thrips attack are the dark spots (droppings) and also spots on the leaves that turn from pale silver to corky. These are formed from cells which have been sucked out and then fill with air. Thrips lay their eggs with an ovipositor in the leaves or other plant tissues, and their development depends on the temperature and light levels. 10–12 generations a year are possible in some cases. For orchids two species are particularly troublesome: the western flower thrips and the banded greenhouse thrips.
Thrips attack can lead to stunted growth and deformities in stems and buds. Control by using coloured sticky traps, and suitable insecticides. Biological control using beneficial insects is also an option.

㉝ Spider mites
One of the most serious of orchid pests, spider mites are not hard to detect. The

first signs are pinpoint paler spots on the leaves – spider mites suck out individual cells which then fill with air. The spots then get larger as the infestation increases, the leaves turn dull yellow and eventually dry off. In really bad cases the leaves and flowers can be covered with a fine web. The mites themselves are only up to 0.5 mm (¹⁄₅₀ in) long, yellow to orange or greenish, and you need a lens to see them properly. Spider mites are mostly found on the undersides of the leaves and they move rather slowly. They prefer high temperatures and dry air. They are often only detected late, by which time the plant is already damaged. Orchids at most risk are *Cymbidium*, *Cattleya*, *Miltonia* and all other soft-leaved genera, but also *Phalaenopsis*. One of the most frequent is the red spider mite which breeds fastest at a high temperature around 27°C (81°F) and low humidity. Buds and flowers are also attacked by spider mites. Apply 'first aid' by removing badly affected leaves and flowers and apply a special spider mite acaricide. Biological control is also sometimes effective.

㉞ Soft-skinned mites
These are elongated, transparent mites, 0.2–0.3 mm (²⁄₁₀₀₀–³⁄₁₀₀₀ in) long, and are therefore very hard to spot. They breed at high temperature and humidity and prefer growing tissues. Their feeding can cause deformed leaves and stems. These light-sensitive pests often affect *Paphiopedilum* or *Dendrobium*, and expert advice should be sought.

㉟ Whiteflies
Small white insects about 1.5 mm (³⁄₅₀ in) long, with rather long, white wings, these

▲ ㉙ The worst enemies of many orchids are mealybugs. Not only are they difficult to remove, they can also spread rapidly on houseplants.

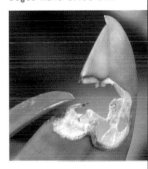

▼ ㉚ Slug or snail damage to a young leaf remains visible for a long time, but is not dangerous after the edges have dried off.

▼ ㉝ Spider mites are easy to spot, and a web indicates a bad attack. Specialist acaricides should be used to treat this problem.

▲ ㉟ If an orchid has whitefly, inspect other houseplants nearby. Soft-leaved houseplants are usually the first to succumb.

are usually found under the leaves of soft-leaved orchids. They tend to take to the air when the plant is moved. The scale-like larvae sit on the undersides of the leaves. These are colourless at first, becoming yellow-green and eventually covered in a white powder. Like scale insects, they create honeydew. Treat with repeated doses of insecticide. Biological control with beneficial insects can be very successful.

㊱ Viruses

A virus attack is not necessarily fatal for orchids. However, viruses do deform leaves and flowers, change colours and hinder growth. But they are hard to diagnose and problems with nutrition, light, water, temperature or humidity are often wrongly blamed for causing the symptoms. If in doubt, get the symptoms analysed by an expert.
Viruses are very small and are only visible under the electron microscope.

They have no metabolism of their own and reproduce inside the cells of their host. *Cymbidium* mosaic virus and *Odontoglossum* ring-spot virus are fairly easy to identify, and these cause pale patches in the tissues. They affect mainly the young leaves. The pale spots later blacken and become indented, first on the undersides of the leaves, later above as well. In severe cases the infected leaves fall off. Spots or striped patches on the upper leaf surface indicate a rhabdovirus. In bad cases the affected tissues dry out, and pale grey, discrete, sunken patches develop, not usually on the undersides. This can lead to fungal infection, and is impossible to treat. Viruses are highly contagious and can only be prevented by hygienic conditions. Care should therefore be taken with knives, scissors, hands, insects, water, and with plant remains and pots. Disinfect with heat or a horticultural cleaning fluid. Dead plants should be removed or destroyed.

▼ ㊱ Virus infections can be hard to detect. This *Cattleya* leaf shows typical damage. Seek expert advice, isolate suspicious cases, and disinfect tools.

Index

Picture credits
All photos by Jörn Pinske except for:
Becherer: 1, 21, 25 above l, 25 above r, 26 above, 27, 48, 51 upper r, 54/55, 63 r, 66/67, 74 above, 78/79, 81 below, 86 above, 110/111, 112 l, 133 below, 137 above, 138 below, 138 middle, 139 above
Bieker: 2/3, 33 middle, 44/45, 80 r, 100/101, 120 above
Eisenbeiss: 90 above, 105 above, 118/119, 129
above l
Hagen: 16 below r, 32 above r, 35 below l, 58
above, 80 l, 91 above r, 98 below
Henseler: 140 above
Krieger: 64 below, 139 above
Redeleit: 91 l, 96 r, 99, 113 upper l
Romeis: 11 above, 30/31, 32 above, 33 below, 34 upper l, 46 above, 47 above, 56 l, 56 r, 72, 81 middle, 81 above, 88/89, 92
above, 93 below, 95, 104 above, 113 above r, 113 below, 124/125
Röth: 10, 13 above, 17 r, 22 r, 23 below, 87 below, 128, 129 above, 133 above
Strauß: 6/7, 33 above, 36, 37 below, 59 above r, 68, 82, 90 below, 102, 103 below, 120 below l, 122, 126 l
Weigl: 15 above, 106 below, 108 below, 116, 129 below r

Design and layout: fuchs_design, Riemerling

Jacket: Anja Masuch, Puchheim, Munich

Jacket photos: front, Ulrike Romeis; back, Josef Bieker

Original German language edition:
© 2005 BLV Buchverlag GmbH & Co.KG, Munich

English language edition:
© 2005 Transedition Ltd, Oxford

This edition published in 2005 by Advanced Marketing (UK) Ltd, Bicester, Oxfordshire

ISBN 1 903938 81 3
Printed and bound in China